New Techniques
for

Winning
Jury
Trials

New Techniques
for
Winning
Jury
Trials

New Techniques for Winning Jury Trials illustrates how jurors decide cases and shows you how to persuade those jurors to vote for you. Credibility, appearance, and demeanor may be just as important to your jury as a technically perfect expert witness.

This book will show you how to . . .

- **Recognize and strike** jurors who will damage your case.
- **Effectively use demonstrative evidence** to increase the jurors' retention by 50%.
- **Integrate psychological and sociological concepts** into your opening and closing statements.
- **Apply these techniques** in both civil and criminal trials.

Copy editor: Lucy A. Paschke

Published by AB Publications
6705 Woodedge Road
Minneapolis, MN 55364

CONTENTS

CHAPTER 3
PRETRIAL PREPARATION

CHAPTER 4

ABOUT THE AUTHOR

Dr. Rasicot is a professional trial consultant from Minneapolis, Minnesota. As a trial consultant, he assists attorneys with their case work-up, voir dire questions and in-court evaluations, demonstrative evidence, and opening/closing statements.

He is considered one of the top authorities in the country on nonverbal communications. As a psychologist, sociologist, and former university professor, he developed and taught graduate and undergraduate courses in interpersonal communications.

The success of his methods has earned him media coverage throughout the United States. In addition to his trial work, he lectures nationally for law firms, law schools, and various legal organizations. He has been featured in *Newsweek, Congressional Quarterly,* the law section of *The New York Times,* and is included in the *Who's Who in American Law.*

Dr. Rasicot has been featured in trial programs in more than thirty-six states, including the ABA National Convention, U.S. Department of Justice and Harvard Law School.

PREFACE

This book demonstrates how to select a favorable jury and how to effectively present a legal case to a lay jury. Attorneys know that the outcome of the trial is directly related to their ability to effectively communicate their facts to the jury.

Successful trial attorneys understand that juries decide cases by receiving and interpreting information from the verbal and the nonverbal phases of the trial. The verbal segments focus on the legal presentation of the case (documents, questioning, evidence). The nonverbal segments focus on the social dynamics of the case (dress, demeanor, credibility). This book illustrates how jurors respond to your presentation of your case. It shows side-by-side examples of positive and negative trial techniques. Courtroom communication becomes more effective when the verbal and the nonverbal segments of the trial are integrated into a clear, concise, central theme.

This book shows how sociological, psychological, and legal concepts can be orchestrated to improve an attorney's courtroom presentation. It illustrates how to recognize and communicate with the four personality types.

My jury selection system combines nonverbal information with verbal responses in order to assess favorable and unfavorable jurors. The system demonstrates which individual personality types are most favorable for a case and how to communicate with the combination of personalities that constitutes a jury.

After years as a trial consultant, I recognize common problem areas for which trial attorneys request assistance. Attorneys know these areas are vital to trial work but are unable to find effective training programs to help them improve these skills. This book is specifically designed to address these problem areas.

CHARTS

ACKNOWLEDGEMENTS

I wish to thank all of the attorneys, judges, and jurors who have helped me, either directly or indirectly, in the writing of this book.

Special recognition is extended to Hennepin County District Judge Chester Durda whose invaluable support and encouragement has been very helpful.

To my parents, Flo and Don, thanks for all of your patience and understanding.

James F. Rasicot

ACKNOWLEDGMENTS

THE LAWYER

A difficult task, that of the Bar,
But a vital part of the justice system.
Working within all the limitations of the Law,
Hoping juries listen to facts, not just their whims.

A lawyer-prosecution or defense,
Spending hours or days to prepare their case,
And maybe, just maybe, the case will make sense,
To judge and jury as you stand face to face.

All too often, no matter the verdict,
The lawyers get second guessed by public and peers.
If they had done it - a far different edict,
As they criticize and weigh - Monday morning seers.

To every lawyer we offer a tip of the hat,
For the career you've chosen, to help all mankind.
When nothing makes sense, just remember that,
Without you, justice and fairness would be hard to find.

Thomas Guthery
Poet, Friend of
James Rasicot

New Techniques
for
Winning
Jury
Trials

- Perspiration
- Preparation
- Presentation

Chapter **1**

OVERVIEW

INTRODUCTION

Law schools traditionally have done an excellent job training attorneys in the technical aspects of trial preparation but a poor job of teaching communication skills. Communication between attorneys is effective because the terminology is the same, but when you must interact with "outsiders" you should adjust your communication style. When presenting a case to a judge rather than to a lay jury, for example, the successful attorney may have a different style and strategy.

The material contained in this book will assist you in both understanding and visualizing basic principles of communication. The information introduced in this book was taken from the social sciences and was tested in the legal environment, combining the needs of both into a practical, usable system.

In a trial, committing minor mistakes gives free ammunition to your adversary. It can be compared to committing an error in every inning of a baseball game; you may still win the game (even though they have nine additional "outs") but you have far more to overcome. I prefer to force my adversaries to win the game on their own merits, not my mistakes. **Errors in dress, demeanor, and space and time usage may seem like minor points, but small holes sink large ships.**

My method of visually assessing jurors has been developed and proven to be effective in the courtroom environment and incorporates original research findings. I do not claim to have created a perfect jury selection system. There is no perfectly reliable way to predict twelve persons' future behavior; human nature is too complex. Regardless, we must attempt to continually improve selection systems in an effort to arrive at the "best jury." I am aware, of course, that there are as many theories of jury selection as there are attorneys. I trust, however, that with practice you will find my system accurate and useful.

Obviously we have to take our clients and the facts of the case as they are, but how we present our team and the facts will either increase or decrease their credibility with and influence on the jury.

COMMUNICATION BASICS

The process of communication can be likened to a Gestalt pattern: individual elements by themselves carry limited information. A Gestalt pattern of communication means that the combination of elements in total is worth more than the sum of its parts. In the courtroom, for instance, you may have carefully researched your case, skillfully selected the jurors, and delivered a word-perfect opening statement. If, however, the opening statement is delivered inappropriately, the effectiveness of the total picture is diminished. It would also be counterproductive to have the three above-mentioned parts not focused on the same theme.

All parts of the trial, visual as well as verbal, must support a central theme consistent with the trial goal. Obviously, it is detrimental to dress in an upper-class fashion, speak in middle-class language and manner, and select a jury from the lower class. That is why image must also be a part of the trial strategy. Each communication error takes five or six actions of commensurate positive value to even the score. For that reason, two or three negative individual habits can make the difference between excellence and mediocrity over a long legal career.

Communication is a three-step process of giving, receiving, and understanding information and will occur only when all three steps have been completed. The most neglected of these is the final one—understanding. Generally we give the message and assume it has been understood. Millions of dollars in lost productivity occurs daily as a result of this miscommunication.

There are two kinds of communication attorneys use while in trial:

1. *Verbal.* If the jury does not understand your case, your chances of being successful are greatly diminished. Therefore the key to an effective trial is to fulfill the legal requirements in such a way that a lay jury will not only understand it but also will find it interesting. This is a tremendous challenge in long, technical cases. (Brilliance is the ability to make a complicated subject seem simple.) Successful attorneys do not try to impress the jury with their intelligence; rather they concentrate on assisting the

jury to understand the complexities of the case. They speak a language that jurors can comprehend—commonly understood terminology. They will never "speak down" to jurors or patronize them. If plain speaking is combined into the Gestalt (total) pattern of communication, understanding and rapport should occur.

2. **Nonverbal.** People give out information about themselves by their dress, demeanor, and numerous other nonverbal factors. Better understanding of nonverbal meanings increases our communications with people. This is parallel to verbal communication in that the more words we understand the better our interaction with a wider group of people. If the process of communication is to be completed (information is received and understood by jurors), it must be expressed in words, concepts, and visual images that are easily comprehended. When technical language is received but has not been (or has only partially been) understood, the case is weakened. Conversely, when you integrate both verbal and nonverbal aspects of communication to make messages understandable, the power of the messages multiplies.

JURORS' BACKGROUNDS

There are four important things to remember about jurors: (1) they know nothing about the law; it is your task to inform them of the legal principles involved in your case; (2) they know nothing about your case; you must educate them on the facts of your case; (3) they do not care about you, so you must somehow get their empathy; and (4) they do not care about your opponent either.

Although jurors have common sense, they probably know nothing about the legal system. It is important that you explain how the legal system works as the trial proceeds. You cannot depend upon the judge or opposing counsel to explain the legal principles involved in your case. You must want to be the one who explains the legal system to your jurors. For example, if your case involves the concept of burden of proof, you want the jury to understand that legal concept. If you are defense counsel, you want the jury to understand that the legal system dictates that the prosecution present its case first and the defense then responds. Anything about the legal system you feel is important for the jury to know you must explain.

The jurors know nothing about your case. This seems obvious, but after years preparing and immersing yourself in your case it is easy to forget that others do not know even the basic facts. It is your responsibility to inform the jury of the facts of your case. You do not want opposing counsel to inform the jury of your case; you do not want the jury to guess at or assume the facts of your case. If there is anything you want the jury to know about your case, you have to communicate it to them.

Jurors do not necessarily care about your client, your case, or you. It is your responsibility to get the jury on your side. You know that the farther you are from a person the less you care about that person. For example, if you read in the newspaper that John Smith was mugged and shot, you may momentarily feel sympathy for him, but you move on to the next newspaper article and forget about John Smith. You do not know John Smith, were not involved in the incident, and your mind moves on to something else. If, however, John Smith is your neighbor or friend, you would feel strongly about the incident. It is the same with the jury. When the jurors first come into the courtroom, they do not care about you and they do not care about your client. In some cases it is easier to persuade the jury to care about your case. For example, if your client is a badly injured plaintiff, it would be easier to arouse the empathy of the jury than if you were defending a client charged with murder. But even if the case looks bad for your client, you still would like the jurors to feel for you and your client. If you cannot persuade them to feel for your client, then you have to enlist their feelings for you.

Jurors do not necessarily care about your opponent's case either. Generally in criminal cases people will side with the police or the state. They make their decision based on fear. Decisions based on fear fulfill two needs for jurors: (1) revenge for the victim of the crime, and (2) they feel it makes the streets safer for them if the put the "bad guy" in prison. In our country we have a presumption of guilt. The majority of people who come into the courtroom look at the defendant and think that if he is not guilty he would not be there. If you are defending a criminal case you need to know how to turn that fear around to your advantage, even though fear is the strongest of human emotions.

THE JURORS' JOB

There are two basic components in any jury trial, whether criminal or civil: truth and justice. Finding truth and justice is the job of the jurors. They have to decide what happened and they have to decide how justice will be served. You may think these are simple decisions: the jury either finds for you or it finds for your opponent. But there are four versions of truth in any case upon which the jury can decide. There is not just your truth and opposing counsel's truth.

FOUR TRUTHS, FOUR JUSTICES

The first version of truth is the absolute truth. Absolute truth is what really happened. Sometimes absolute truth and your facts are the same. The ideal situation would be if the absolute truth, your facts, and the jury's perception of the case are the same. Your job is to convince the jury that your case is the absolute truth.

The second version of truth is what your team says happened. The third version of truth is your opponent's version of the facts. And the fourth version of truth is what the jury feels happened. In some cases you have your version of the facts, opposing counsel has their version of the facts, and when the verdict is announced, you find that the jury has another version of the facts that may be a combination of your and your opponent's facts.

After the jurors decide the facts of your case they still must decide upon justice. Justice is a subjective term. For your client who has lost a leg, justice may mean two million dollars. For you, the attorney, justice may mean one million dollars. For a juror, who knows neither you nor your client and may never see you again after the trial, justice may mean two hundred thousand dollars. What is right is a personal, subjective decision. And therefore there are four versions of justice: (1) absolute justice that would come from the deity; (2) your justice; (3) the opposing side's justice; and (4) the jury's justice.

Because of the four versions of truth and justice it is important to know your jurors. The jurors' perceptions of truth and justice will depend upon their personalities and their backgrounds. When you are facing the voir dire process you want to select people who will see truth and justice as you and your client do. That is the basic key to success in your trial.

How do you decide what jurors to pick for your trial? Ninety-nine percent of lawyer say that they pick jurors based on their "gut feelings." That is how we all make some decisions. But some lawyers are better at this "gut feeling" than others. What I address in this book is how you can be better at making these "gut decisions."

In any trial there are really two trials occurring: the verbal (what people hear) and the nonverbal (what people see). You must prepare for both of these trials. Lawyers are usually prepared only for the verbal trial. You talk to your witnesses, you have every fact down. But how many lawyers think about the visual trial? For example, how do you dress your client for the best possible impact on the jury? How do you want to present yourself? Your witnesses? The two most important things to remember in a jury trial are credibility and impact. If your team does not have credibility and impact so that the jury will remember it, you will have problems. Remember, people subconsciously go by their "gut feelings," by what they feel is right.

THE VERBAL AND NONVERBAL TRIALS

Communication is the most important aspect of the trial. During face-to-face communication, 60 percent of the total message is transmitted nonverbally, 30 percent is transmitted through voice inflection, and only 10 percent of the total message is interpreted from the words themselves. Decisions by the jury are based upon the total communication received from both the verbal and the nonverbal trials.

Communicators refer to this relationship as the "60+30+10 interactional formula." As you can see, 90 percent of the total meaning of our information is interpreted nonverbally. Voice inflection and visual demeanor are the most important clues to your feelings and attitudes about your words. You can tell someone to "shake my hand" in such a way as to give a strong order, a submissive request, or question the very act itself, simply by how you present the words. The attorney who wins the verbal trial but loses the nonverbal trial has a diminished chance of winning overall. Communication with jurors increases when you ensure that the visual and verbal aspects of the trial complement and support each other.

The courtroom is slightly different from most social settings in that by design more emphasis is placed on verbalization. Remember though, lawyers and judges are accustomed to this concentrated focus because they work in the environment, but a juror is a stranger to the setting and is more accustomed to being visually stimulated. Therefore it becomes essential to concentrate on both aspects.

In older and more traditional cultures, such as Japan, people acquire the meanings and commensurate responses of nonverbal communication as they learn the language. Nonverbal communications are universal but vary from culture to culture. North America represents a collection of people from all over the world; it possesses the residue of hundreds of different language systems. As a nation, the United States is still developing nonverbal habits. Luckily, nonverbal communication is relatively uniform in its basic forms, although you must be careful to pick out unique cultural differences. It therefore becomes critical to understand the fundamentals of nonverbal communication in order to effectively adjust to others. The courtroom attorney, on any given day, may be speaking to jurors of any number of different cultural backgrounds.

As a general rule, communication is most complete between equals. Persons of similar racial, gender, ethnic, religious, or class backgrounds have the best chance of being understood by each other. It is the responsibility of the communicators, however, to make themselves understood.

The language of lawyers is the language of the upper middle class. As a nation of immigrants we do not have a single class system that crosscuts all of America. Class differences can vary tremendously from one community to the next. An upper-middle-class speech pattern in one area of the United States frequently may be interpreted as a lower-middle-class pattern in another part of the country. Attorneys who emphasize their upper-middle-class orientation too strongly will tend to lose cultural identification with middle- and lower-class jurors; a balance is necessary. Fortunately, most middle- and lower-middle-class persons have upper-middle-class listening habits along with their lower- and middle-class speech patterns. If this were not the case, the jury system would be under far more pressure than it is at present.

FIVE AREAS OF PERSONAL ASSESSMENT

Most communication occurs through nonverbal signals. Words are used to transmit ideas, while the nonverbal indicators such as demeanor or voice inflection transmit your attitudes and cultural values about those ideas or information.

In interpersonal relationships there are five basic areas that you use to assess others and others use to assess you; each one will be explained in detail in chapter 2.

DRESS

We usually decide whether we like, dislike, or feel neutral about another person within the first few minutes of initial contact. This is what we call our "first impression." We know this impression is of paramount importance and has long-lasting effects. The lawyer's team's appearance is, therefore, a critical indicator throughout the trial, but particularly during the first day. Image basics include race, gender, dress, jewelry, body build, hairstyle, facial hair, makeup, posture, demeanor, and numerous other personal indicators. Dress plays a very large part in first impressions. Dress is also a two-dimensional image: what clothing is worn and how these clothes are worn. Illustrations (1.1a) and (1.1b) represent the same model, illustrated to portray a highly dissimilar personal image created by simply wearing different clothing. The upper-middle-class image is portrayed in (1.1a), while illustration (1.1b) is typical of a blue-collar worker. This imagery is so standardized in American culture that you may accuse me of being trite for its inclusion. Nevertheless, compare illustrations (1.1c) and (1.1d): the same model wearing similar clothes. The sloppily dressed illustration reflects the image of a less authoritative person who is uncaring or that of a person who is uninformed about dress etiquette. Sloppy or inappropriate attire greatly reduces your or your witness's ability to command authority and maintain credibility.

CHANGING PERSONAL IMAGES BY TYPE OF DRESS

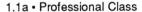

1.1a • Professional Class   1.1b • Working Class

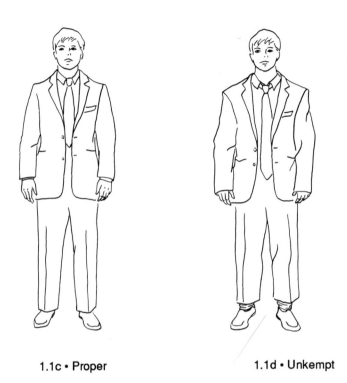

1.1c • Proper   1.1d • Unkempt

BODY LANGUAGE (KINESICS)

The way in which people sit, stand, and walk are valuable indicators in assessing their personalities and interest levels. Compare the alert, confident, and open demeanor of illustration (1.2a) with the uninterested, bored, and closed demeanor of illustration (1.2b). Actually the man in illustration (1.2b) may just be tired or preoccupied with the day's events. Nevertheless, he is signaling to at least some of the jury members that he is bored and uninterested. Whether or not this is the impression he wants to give is immaterial. The image he actually presents is interpreted by others who then react to their assessment of him.

DEMEANOR

1.2a
- Open
- Alert
- Confident

1.2b
- Closed
- Bored
- Uninterested

DEMEANOR

1.2c
- Open
- Relaxed
- Assured

1.2d
- Closed
- Tense
- Withdrawn

1.2e
- Open
- Relaxed
- Interested

1.2f
- Closed
- Tense
- Pensive

Women have a culturally learned tendency to occupy less space than men as well as a tendency to close or cross their arms when they become tired. Compare the open, confident, and relaxed demeanor of illustration (1.2c) with the closed, lacking-in-confidence, and tense demeanor of (1.2d). Which identically dressed person is most believable, most confident, most powerful?

If we change the woman in illustrations (1.2c) and (1.2d) to a sitting position we can observe the difference between an open, confident demeanor and that of a person who appears perplexed or unsure of herself. Again, the woman in illustration (1.2f) may just be tired, but she appears to be tense and unsure of herself.

SPACE USAGE (PROXEMICS)

How you use the space around you is a clue to your personality and your relationships. Space can be divided into two main groups: social and territorial, and into two planes: horizontal and vertical. Social space refers to how you control the space that surrounds you as you move through society.

The four zones of social space are the intimate, personal, social, and public. These zones will vary by culture and gender. It is important, nevertheless, to know the basic differences in order to observe the reactions to others as you enter and leave their "space bubbles." If you are close enough to kiss or hug another person, you have entered the intimate zone (0–1 foot). The personal zone (1–3 feet) is close enough to put a hand on the other's shoulder; the social zone (3–4 feet) is within handshaking distance; and the public zone starts at four to five feet away.

Illustration (1.3a) depicts the second woman at a handshaking or social distance from the man. In chapter 2 I will elaborate on some of the rules governing the use of horizontal space. At this point let it suffice to recognize that "social" distance rules should normally be observed when meeting clients and witnesses or when approaching jurors.

HORIZONTAL SPACE ZONES

1.3a
• Personal
• Social
• Public

Vertical space is especially important because it can be used to gain power and authority. Teachers standing over students, judges who occupy the highest courtroom elevation, and adults towering over children all convey an image of authority and power.

Illustration (1.3b) represents the natural height advantage that men typically have over women. The woman, however, has neutralized this advantage in (1.3c) and has gained the advantage in (1.3d). Height power is commonly observed in the courtroom by lawyers approaching the witnesses and jurors. Misuse of vertical and horizontal power dimensions may be interpreted as coercion and intimidation; it should be used only when that is your conscious intent.

Jurors' territorial space should be carefully observed by all who approach the jury box. Placing a hand on their railing or handing objects into their space should be done as carefully as if you were moving about the jurors' homes.

VERTICAL SPACE

1.3b • Man has Height Power

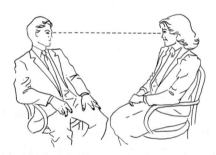

1.3c • Height Power Neutralized

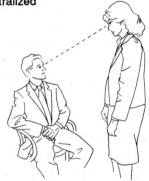

1.3d • Woman has Height Power

TIME

How long we talk, how long we permit others to talk without interruption, and how long we remain in conversation provides us with additional personality insights. Scheduling around recesses, lunch breaks, and particular times of the day occasionally can be used as part of your overall strategy. Attention spans are generally best early in the morning and early in the trial. Notetaking will be highest during these periods. As the trial wears on, notetaking decreases. Most of the time notetaking gives an advantage to the prosecutor/plaintiff.This obviously is a handicap for the defense. When jurors take their notes into the juryroom they tend to rely on those more than their memories.

In illustration (1.4b) the woman is showing indifference in contrast to (1.4a). The man in (1.4b) has used up his profitable time, and the longer he speaks the more negative her attitude will become.

The attention span of Americans has been shortened drastically over the years as a result of a faster paced society. In a sense, as when watching television, viewers are waiting for the commercials to occur. After seventeen to twenty minutes, the likelihood of jurors completely processing what they hear rapidly diminishes. Long opening and closing statements or long cross-examinations are most effective if the jury's attention span is taken into consideration. Longer presentations are more effective if one or two crescendos are reached before the finale. Seasoned attorneys will frequently follow a pattern of building drama and dropping off, building again and dropping off again, building drama and terminating. Using this technique can increase attention spans, but this too has its limitations. Direct and cross-examination may last several hours, with the jury remaining relatively attentive if there is new material and the interaction of different people to break up the time. Contrast this with opening and closing statements in which one person is doing all of the talking with no other direct interaction.

TIME USAGE

1.4a • Mutual interest

1.4b • Male interest and female indifference

VERBAL IMAGE

While persons speak we assess their verbal skill and conceptual level of conversation. Middle-class language patterns, preferably patterned after the jurors' own locale, will carry more credibility than language patterns that contain poor grammar, mispronounced words, or slang. Attorneys who assist the jury by clarifying definitions and technical terminology increase personal credibility with the jury. Positive rapport is gained by providing explanations, using courtesy statements that clarify procedure or expectations, and treating listeners as intellectual equals.

CULTURAL NORMS

Cultural norms teach "value" and "feeling" messages that almost everyone understands. Consequently, a conscious use of those messages is an integral part of a successful overall strategy for the trial. In the social process of learning to work in groups, you incorporate thousands of rules that guide your behavior toward others. The behavioral guidance comes from a combination of emotions and values as well as from words and visual images that are all shaped and made complete by cultural norms. Feelings and emotions tend to affect your decisions more than conscious reasoning. If you violate the normative expectations of jurors, the most logical arguments will not be effective. Decisions are made emotionally because emotions control which facts are weighed the heaviest and which facts are blocked out in the final decision-making process. The attorney who violates the norm of "fairness" during the trial, for example, is rarely successful.

Overkill. Let us take the example of cross-examination for the purpose of discrediting a witness. Most jurors possess a cultural rule that permits this discrediting process to continue only to a given point. Beyond this point, sympathy is elicited for the witness. If you continue to attack a witness beyond this point (overkill) you will be transferring negative feelings to you. This same principle can be illustrated by using boxing as an example. People who view boxing accept the fact that a person may get hurt during the bout. But if one boxer continues to beat up his helpless opponent without the bout being stopped, the original competitive spirit of the audience turns to sympathy for the loser and disdain for their former hero. You can effectively discredit facts or actions but not the person. When the facts are discredited properly, jurors will impeach the witness themselves. By leading the jurors to a conclusion that they are permitted to make for themselves, you avoid triggering sympathy for the witness.

Over Objecting. This violates our cultural rule regarding fair communications. Making objections too frequently becomes annoying. It distracts the jurors' attention and gives the impression that the attorney is attempting to cover the facts. A careful reading of the jury's nonverbal communication is necessary to fully assess the impact you are making. Some objections must be made for the record regardless of the jury's reactions, but numerous borderline objections are what I am stressing here.

Put downs. Derogatory inferences about race, religion, gender, and occupations are obviously negatively received by the jury as well as by the court. You must be careful to keep your prejudices out of the trial process. These feelings most often come up in a heated trial, during either examinations or closing statements.

Nonpersons. A nonperson is a person we view as an object or as a service provider. For instance, people in elevators view each other as nonpersons, as do people standing in line or people with doctors, salesmen, and clerks. Lawyers, clients, judges, and individual jurors are initially viewed as nonpersons—performing a function but with no emotional bond among participants. The quicker you and your client shed the "nonperson" role with the jury the better your chances are for success. It is much easier for the jury to sentence an "object" to prison than it is to sentence "John" to prison. It feels better to give "Martha" one hundred thousand dollars than it does to give a "client" the same amount of money. As you can see, emotions guide you again to your final decision. Visual images are assessed emotionally, and the difference between a one million dollar award and a two million dollar award is most often the degree of emotional involvement with the client/attorney.

Because of our fast-paced and crowded world, all societies need nonpersons in order to function smoothly. For instance, people in an elevator maintain certain distances between each other and face the door to eliminate eye contact. Even though they are invading each other's personal space zones, and in fact may even be touching one another, they are relaxed because they are surrounded by "nonpersons." One person can change the entire setting by entering the elevator, standing with his back to the door, and looking directly at the other people. He now becomes a human being, causing the others to feel more threatened and stressful. Some people will actually get off at the next floor to relieve this increase in tension.

Society needs nonpersons, but you do not want the jury to view your client as such. This is why it is important to refer to your client, if possible, by his or her first name and never say "my client." Conversely, your adversary is referred to as "counsel" and his or her client as "defendant" or "plaintiff."

Appearance. Our cultural expectations are that lawyers and judges wear certain clothes, have an upper-class image, be intelligent, and be verbally smooth. If as a male lawyer you wish to appear in court with a long ponytail and earrings, you may certainly do so. But recognize that you are violating the norm and you run the risk of creating a negative image in most jurors' minds. We all have a personal and a public image. If what we choose to do with our personal image begins to interfere with our public image (job), we have a problem that we must solve. If a male wants to dress as a woman and does so in his home on his personal time, that may create few problems, but if he chooses to wear women's clothing as a business executive, he may be eliciting negative responses from others. You must decide where your personal preferences stop and when your client's best interests are being damaged.

One of the easiest ways to gain courtroom credibility is to observe all cultural rules of fairness. People of all classes, races, and genders have, throughout most of their lives, picked up on the meaning and nuances of fairness. Increasing awareness and positive use of cultural rules for more effective verbal and nonverbal courtroom communication is a major goal of this text.

REAL VERSUS IDEAL

In the legal system, as well as in almost all other aspects of society, we have two styles of looking at the system. We have the philosophers who live in a world they feel should exist, and we have the practitioners who adjust to the world as it is. We can all relate (in different degrees) to each side.

Guilt versus innocence. We are culturally taught to believe that a criminal trial will prove whether or not the accused is guilty or innocent of the crime. We know this is not true; a trial only shows "guilty" or "not guilty" (which we refer to as "not proven guilty"). Innocence does not have to be proven. If the prosecutor cannot prove guilt, the accused is set free. This idea is brought up because jurors want to know who committed the crime if the defendant did not (or at the very least they want a theory of who did it and why). The ideal trial would prove either that the defendant is guilty or innocent. That is what the jury expects. As a lawyer, you must live with the actual facts and adjust to satisfy the jury. If you are a defense lawyer in a criminal case and you give the jurors an idea or theory of who else committed the crime, it is easier for them to find your client not guilty. Psychologically they want the problem solved. If the defendant did not do it, who did?

Images. In theory, dress, demeanor, and sociological factors other than the actual case facts should be superfluous to the determination of guilt or innocence of the defendant. These sociological factors also should not determine whether or not a client is awarded one million dollars or two million dollars. The facts alone should merit the verdicts. Ideally that is correct, but as a practicality a great many cases are decided upon social factors. It is important to recognize the tremendous influence of social factors on trial outcomes, and in order to become successful these factors must be incorporated into your overall trial strategy.

Jurors' biases. Ideally the jurors decide the case based entirely on the facts. Facts fit into the reading of the law without personal judgments becoming involved. Very few jurors consciously decide a case based upon their own biases; however, most jurors subconsciously decide a case through their personal rationalization of the facts throughout the case. Their subconscious filters what they wish to hear and do not wish to hear.

Humor. Humor should be used very sparingly (if at all) in the courtroom. When jurors are asked to interrupt their lives to sit in judgment in order to assist justice, they want to feel the case is very important. Humor can be a time bomb if it is misused, and only the most skillful lawyer should use it as a tool. The rule is, if you are skillful enough to use humor as a tool, you are smart enough to stay away from it. It is important to have a sense of humor and adjust to a unique situation but then return to the seriousness of your client's one chance to prevail. Levity should be eliminated during breaks as well as in the courtroom. Jurors usually take their work very seriously, and the lawyers should show as much concern during the trial as they do during the final moments when they ask for the verdict.

SUMMARY

The practice of trial law represents a communication process that can be significantly enhanced by following a few sound principles derived from the social sciences. The material in this chapter was not all-inclusive but was meant to serve only as an introduction; it will be elaborated and explained in much greater detail in the next six chapters.

The foundation of chapter 1 supports the basic premise that trial lawyers are most effective when they understand that there are two different trials going on at the same time: the verbal trial (what the jurors hear) and the visual trial (what the jurors see). The verdict reflects information gathered from both trials. Success depends upon winning both trials.

Chapter 2 explains how dress, body language, space, and time usage affects your courtroom presentation.

VISUAL COURTROOM COMMUNICATIONS

DRESS

Dress is the most easily changed part of your appearance. Race and gender are permanently set, but different images can be achieved by adjusting your personal dress to fit your desired image.

Dress rules are as firmly rooted in the norms of American culture as the rules of social etiquette. There are different regional, gender, and age variations, but the basic guidelines will superimpose themselves over these variations. I will cover the fundamental dimensions of dress that are important to the courtroom setting.

The dress continuums for males and females have been simplified (charts I and II) to demonstrate how you can use mix-and-match clothing to achieve the desired courtroom image. By using the combinations from the power continuum, you can select each individual's dress (according to the person's part in the case) and see how it will fit into the team's overall image. As you move downward on the power scale you move upward on the friendliness scale and vice versa. Naturally, you must first determine which particular effect you wish each witness to convey. For instance, expert witnesses need all the power they can get and so they generally dress very formally. A factory worker may look out of character and therefore be a distraction in a three-piece suit with a white shirt.

As you move down the power continuum you are paralleling in social terms the movement from the upper to the lower classes. For obvious reasons I have not covered high fashion or clothing that is strictly for special social purposes because they are not relevant to courtroom situations. Women have slightly more flexibility than men regarding colors and patterns, but like men, when they blatantly break the rules, they pay the penalty.

Regional variations exist from one part of the country to another, but no geographical difference is greater than that which exists between urban and rural areas. If you are unfamiliar with dress in a new area, it is well worth the time to explore local norms.

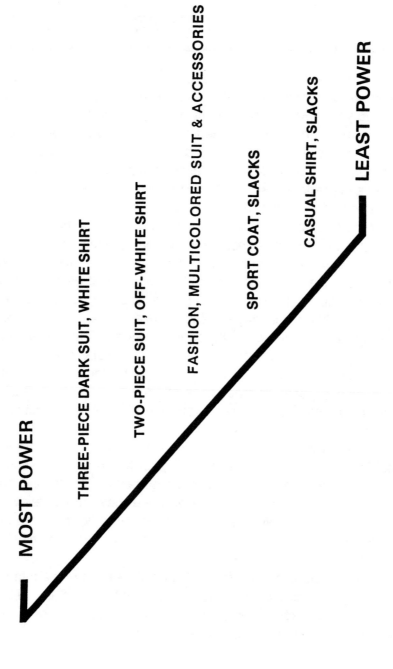

CHART I

POWER DRESS FOR MEN

MOST POWER

THREE-PIECE DARK SUIT, WHITE SHIRT

TWO-PIECE SUIT, OFF-WHITE SHIRT

FASHION, MULTICOLORED SUIT & ACCESSORIES

SPORT COAT, SLACKS

CASUAL SHIRT, SLACKS

LEAST POWER

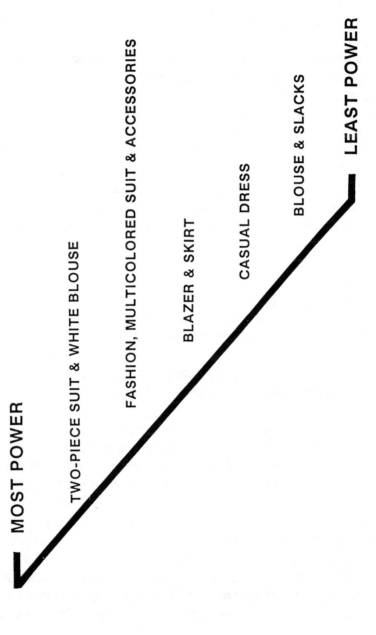

CHART II

POWER DRESS FOR WOMEN

MOST POWER

TWO-PIECE SUIT & WHITE BLOUSE

FASHION, MULTICOLORED SUIT & ACCESSORIES

BLAZER & SKIRT

CASUAL DRESS

BLOUSE & SLACKS

LEAST POWER

As the age of the client or witness increases, so will the normative expectation of increased conservatism. A "twenties" look for a fifty-year-old appears out of place even when other aspects of the dress continuum are followed. When there is a difference between dress and age, similar to what was just suggested, use dress to more accurately assess that person. If a fifty-year-old woman dresses in a miniskirt and a low-cut blouse, she is showing that mentally she considers herself back in her twenties and tends to relate better to that group of people. She will usually have a twenty-year-old decision-making orientation.

Dark colors are associated with higher status. They appear more solid and serious than do the lighter and brighter colors. The four main power colors are blue, gray, brown, and tan. Brown suits test very poorly in the eastern United States but are acceptable in the other regions. Furthermore, favorable ratings of sincerity and competence also accompanied the four basic colors of business clothing.

A recent apparel study by Litigation Sciences examined the impact of the color of attorney's clothing and how it affected the perceptions of approximately 1,000 Los Angeles County jurors. Results show that brown, tan, gray, and dark blue suits, in that color order, increased impressions of power; however, differences were very slight. (Civil Trial Tactics, 1983, 45.) Sports coats tested poorly. You should be careful not to generalize this study to all other geographical areas of the United States.

Contrary to some of the liberalizing dress influences of the 1970s, the decades of the 1980s and 1990s reflect a swing back toward more conservative dress for both men and women. High fashion dress is only appropriate after hours or for special social occasions. In the courtroom, the more noticeable your dress, hair, jewelry, or personal effects the greater the distraction. Distractions should only be used when a special effect is desired. The rule of the courtroom is to dress to project the image that most accurately represents your team's strategy.

An important dress factor to remember is that you can dress "down" after first meetings but not "up." Class position or status is primarily associated with first impressions; you tend to retain the status from the initial dress even though dress image moves down the power continuum during subsequent meetings. If you dress down for the first meeting, you basically retain that initial lower status throughout the trial. Additionally, dressing down carries with it a loss of sincerity and competence that is very hard to recapture. This is why I recommend as a general rule that urban lawyers wear suits and rural lawyers wear sport coats. Rural populations generally dress more casually in their business as well as in their personal lives. Your goal is to relate to the jury and establish credibility at the same time. You never have a second chance to establish a good first impression.

DRESS CONTINUUMS

The amount of power you project through clothing is illustrated by the power dress continuums. Before I trace this relationship, however, a comment about age must be included. Men socially gain age credibility (authority) at about thirty years; women socially gain age authority at about age forty. Both men and women begin to lose age authority about the time of retirement, around sixty-five years. Keeping this variable in mind, dressing up on the power continuum can accelerate age credibility. For instance a twenty-year-old salesman who dresses in a dark suit and white shirt can increase his visual power image, if consistent.

The dress continuum for men and women is very similar. At the top of each power continuum is the three-piece suit with a plain white shirt or blouse, and at the bottom of the continuum are shirts and blouses without jackets.

The power continuum was produced from a standard dress code that has been gradually accepted over a long period of time. It can be used regardless of rapidly changing fashion trends. This is the reason high fashion suits tend to rate third on the scale; tomorrow they may be out of use (leisure suit).

OUTER AND INNER GARMENTS

Outer garments (suit coat, jacket, or blazer) primarily represent a person's status. The inner pieces of clothing such as ties, shirts, blouses, and shoes reflect one's individual personality. In other words, you can take more liberty with your inner garments than you can take with the outer. This does not mean, however, that you have complete license with shirts, blouses, and ties; later discussion in this chapter will clarify these points.

The outer-inner garment differential can be used to tone up or tone down your total dress image (illustrations 2.0a through 2.0j). If you desire the status of a three-piece suit (the outer garment), the image can be softened with an off-white or colored shirt and a more casual tie. On the other hand, if you desire to increase the status of a sport coat, it can be dressed up with a power tie and white shirt.

When you are evaluating jurors, a quick assessment of the inner-outer garment is most essential. Quality of clothing is important in assessing status, as are accompanying items of jewelry, hair styling, and accessories. An expensive three-piece suit with old scuffed shoes gives insight into that person's personality. Conversely, a person in jeans and an athletic jersey who wears a large diamond ring and a very expensive gold watch is also giving you a message.

MALE OUTER GARMENTS POWER CONTINUUM

2.0a • Three-Piece Suit   2.0b • Two-Piece Suit   2.0c • Fashion Suit   2.0d • Sport Coat   2.0e • Jacketless

FEMALE OUTER GARMENTS POWER CONTINUUM

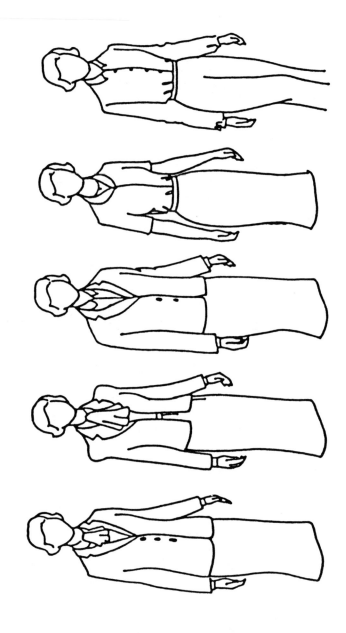

2.0f • Two-Piece Suit 2.0g • Fashion Suit 2.0h • Blazer/Skirt 2.0i • Casual Dress 2.0j • Blouse/Slacks

SHIRTS AND BLOUSES

The man's power shirt continuum proceeds from (1) the plain white shirt, which is most powerful; (2) the plain off-white shirt; (3) the striped shirt; to (4) the plaid shirt. The sequence is similar for women's blouses. Whether blouses are white or off-white, however, their power decreases as they become more ornate. Increasing the size of "frills" decreases power (2.0l). Brightly colored blouses, like shirts, also reduce your power image.

Collared shirts and blouses have more power than uncollared shirts and blouses. Plain collars have the highest degree of power (2.0k). Collar lengths change over time, but medium lengths remain highest on the power scale. Button-down collars are next in the power continuum, with pinned collars coming in third and open collars last. Pinned collars for men are third in power because of the rate at which they move in and out of style.

SHIRTS POWER CONTINUUM

2.0k
- Straight Collar
- Button-Down Collar
- Fashion Pin

2.0l
• Straight Collar
• Rounded Collar, Ornate Buttons
• Frilly Collar and Lacey Front

TIES AND SCARVES

The three basic business ties for men are (1) foulard (geometric designs), (2) club (those with horses, horns, and such), and (3) repp (striped designs). Power tends to be highest with foulard, lowest with stripes, and clubs fall in the middle (2.0m).

Ties for women tend to be more varied and stylish. As a woman's tie or scarf increases in size, the relative power associated with it decreases (2.0n). The effect is similar to that which occurs as you go from a plain white blouse to a frilly colored blouse.

TIES AND SCARVES POWER CONTINUUM

2.0m
• Foulard
• Club
• Repp

2.0n
• Small Tie
• Medium Scarf
• Large Scarf

SHOES AND BOOTS

The plain-toed shoe for both men and women is most powerful (2.0o and 2. 0p). Men's shoes with ties are more powerful than buckled or slip-on styles. Women's enclosed shoes are more powerful than open-toed or open-heeled. The more ornate the shoe becomes the less power it conveys. Elevated heels for men are considered too fashionable for business dress and the wearer loses points. High heels increase a woman's status by adding height and an upper-class image. Boots have inherently less power than dress shoes.

SHOE POWER CONTINUUM

2.0o
• Plain Toed
• Wing Tip
• Loafer

 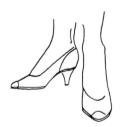 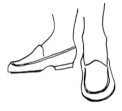

2.0p
• Closed High Heel
• Open High Heel
• Flat

58

Dress boots for men and women follow the same continuum from plain to ornate. Dress boots are generally inappropriate for courtroom lawyers, except in certain western areas where they are considered normal footwear. Again, you need to be cognizant of the different geographical norms. Work boots of any type, sneakers, and deck shoes all carry a lower-class image in the courtroom

JEWELRY

If the team members' clothing, jewelry, hair, or other related features stand out enough to be remembered by jurors, it has been overdone. Expensive or stylish rings, watches, earrings, bracelets, or necklaces that call attention or distract from your demeanor and image should be eliminated. When clients, witnesses, or counsel become nervous there is a tendency to play with jewelry. A fairly safe rule of thumb for men is to limit jewelry to a wedding band or one ring and a watch; for women jewelry should be similarly inconspicuous. Earrings should be small and in good taste without "dangling" or reflecting exotic colors or shapes. Necklaces, if they are worn at all, should be unobtrusive.

Jewelry can tell you quite a bit about a person. Does the person wear jewelry for ornamental purposes (hoop earrings, aesthetic items), for informational purposes (class rings, club pins, birthstone rings), or for functional purposes (watches, medic alert bracelets)? Where does the person wear the jewelry (neck, wrist or anklet bracelets, which fingers have rings)? There is a difference between the married woman who wears a plain gold band, an ornate aesthetic silver band, a one-carat diamond wedding ring, or a children's birthstone wedding ring. Each one has a different way of expressing a relationship through her jewelry

HAIR

As the length of your hair increases your credibility as an authority or professional person diminishes (2.0q). This rule applies to counsel, clients, and witnesses. In our culture we generally associate sexiness with longer hair on women. Women's credibility with men decreases as hair length increases as a result of increased sexual connotations. If a woman prefers long hair, it is advisable to wear it up when she needs to gain power.

Men's hair is socially regarded in much the same way as women's (2.0r). Short hair is masculine and long hair is feminine. Hairstyles for men have lengthened the business cut over the past few years, but the short-around-the-ears style has remained the executive preference. As male hair covers the ears there is a proportional decrease in related social status. To a point, one can wear hair a little longer and compensate with power dress. By the time the hair completely covers the ears, however, the ability to compensate with dress is greatly reduced.

FACIAL HAIR

Facial hair is a negative distraction 90 percent of the time. People are generally not "turned off" by a clean-shaven face, but many have adverse reactions to facial hair.

There are three primary reasons men wear facial hair. Knowing the reasons can be of assistance when assessing personalities. This is another single indicator that, when added to the others, creates a total picture. The three reasons are:

1. To cover up a physical or mental problem. Physically you can use facial hair to cover scars or deformities or to make speech problems less noticeable (hairlip). Mentally you use hair to look older or to hide behind your "mask" of hair.

WOMEN'S HAIR POWER CONTINUUM

2.0q
• Short
• Medium
• Long

MEN'S HAIR POWER CONTINUUM

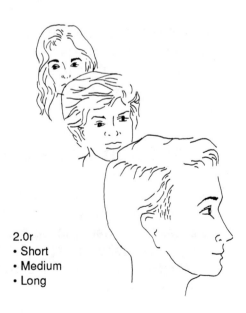

2.0r
• Short
• Medium
• Long

2. To express individuality or group identification. Individuality may be noticed in a handlebar mustache, when the person wants to assert his freedom and originality. Group identification enables a feeling of belonging, as was long hair during the hippie movement for the purpose of separation from the "establishment."

3. To express aggression or machismo. Mustaches make the mouth look less friendly because it appears to have a permanent frown. The horseshoe mustache (as in "Shogun") is the most aggressive.

You will want to weigh the positive and negative aspects of your image and decide what is most effective for your particular situation. Facial hair may be advantageous if it covers a deficiency that is more of a distraction than is the hair or if you simply feel better with it than without.

Sideburns are viewed more negatively as they increase in size and length.

MALE AND FEMALE DRESS DON'TS

Illustrations (2.0s) and (2.0t) represent the extremes of poor "dress" for men and women. Dress is very important when people do not know each other, as in the courtroom setting. Once people know each other and have formed opinions on each other, dress becomes less important.

CLIENT AND WITNESS DRESS

Most clients and witnesses have never been involved in a trial before. Like other aspects of your case, you want to control their dress as much as possible. Answering these three questions will help you to determine how your team should dress: (1) What is this person's role in this case? (2) What does this person feel comfortable wearing? (3) Do we have a formal or informal jury?

DRESS—TWO-SIDED COIN

There are two major reasons why you need to understand how dress affects people: (1) so you know how to dress your team to increase your effectiveness; and (2) so you are able to understand why the jurors are dressed the way they are so you can more accurately evaluate them.

INAPPROPRIATE MALE COURTROOM DRESS

2.0s
- Tennis Shoes
- Sandals
- Unkempt and Long Hair
- Faded Jeans
* Earrings
- Muscle Shirts

INAPPROPRIATE FEMALE COURTROOM DRESS

2.0t
- Thongs
- Headbands
- Gaudy Jewelry
- Open Spike Heels
- Ratted Hairstyles and Hoop Earrings
- Heavy Makeup

BODY LANGUAGE

Body language (kinesics) is culturally learned and usually controlled subconsciously. As children acquire verbal language they also acquire a complete set of body language communicators. The body language of children normally speaks more loudly than their words, especially when vocabularies are limited. Children who cover their ears, turn down the corners of their mouths in a pout, or fall to the floor in a tantrum are using some very explicit body language. As you mature, your body language usually develops with your vocabulary. Verbal language and body language are inextricably mixed by the time you reach adulthood. Every culture in the world has its own pattern of combined verbal and nonverbal signals. America represents the residue of hundreds of these world cultures.

There are two major aspects of body language that I am emphasizing: that which is culturally or subculturally learned and that which is idiosyncratic. Maude Poiret in *Body Talk* uses an idiosyncratic example specific to trial law practice:

> *A now-well-known lawyer who specializes in labor relations recalls that, early in his career, he often was outmaneuvered by opponents who seemed to know exactly when he was bluffing and when he had reached a point where he was determined not to give in. Later, when he was teamed with a more experienced attorney who previously had been an opponent, he learned why his bluffs were so transparent. 'All I had to do was watch your hands,' his former adversary told him. 'Whenever you were bluffing you fondled your wedding ring. When you let go of the ring I knew that I had pushed you as far as you'd go.'*

The independent observation of your opponents and witnesses usually produces similar nonverbal clues.

Recently in a million dollar civil suit, I noticed that our adversary steepled his hands (2.1a) when he was asking questions and listening to positive replies but moved his hands into fists (2.1b) when he was asking questions we felt he was unsure of. Recognizing this idiosyncracy gave us leverage of which we took advantage throughout the trial. Lawyers sometimes give out more information than the witnesses because they feel all eyes are on the witness and they forget about their own part in giving messages.

Effective communicators synchronize body language and verbal communications. One of the masters at integrating verbal and nonverbal communication is Johnny Carson of the "Tonight Show." Carson's humor frequently involves more body language than words. The manner he uses to coordinate body language with verbal interviewing techniques is masterful in the sense that he adjusts his body language for each individual guest.

When you learn to more effectively "read" the visual signals expressed by others, you more quickly and fully comprehend new insights into personality and clues to situational moods such as lying, tension, and confidence. The next eight sections of this chapter will explain different areas of body language assessment. Remember that in order to accurately assess body language it is the total pattern or combination of movements that is meaningful, not one or two isolated movements. One or two movements by themselves may be interpreted in many different ways, but when you look at five or six movements working together it gives you an accurate picture of the person's feelings.

HAND POSITIONS

2.1a • Steepling for Confidence

2.1b • Clasped for Tension

POSTURING

The way you use horizontal and vertical space, either sitting or standing, is part of your demeanor.

Height is perceived as a superior, or dominant, trait in American society. We call this "height power." The taller person is usually associated with more authority. When you are taller than another person you have both a physical and a psychological advantage. Empirical social data has clearly shown that in the business world taller people are hired and promoted more rapidly than shorter people. Culturally, we expect the person with the most authority to dominate the vertical plane. For example, the judge is higher in the courtroom setting, and the teacher often stands before seated students.

In courtroom settings, where attorneys are permitted to move somewhat freely around the courtroom, height power can be used for specific effects. For example, a lawyer can show dominance over hostile witnesses by standing on the witness box steps, thus having the distinct advantage of being above them. This act is subtly aggressive and you can instantly feel the tension generated. Judges who are aware of this fact may restrict those movements of attorneys that may border on subtle intimidation. In the Minneapolis area, almost all questioning is done from the lawyer's table unless there is a specific reason for approaching the witnesses (handing them documents or discussing exhibits). Several years ago, in a heated slander suit, our adversary stood up and approached the witness for cross-examination. He began asking his questions two feet from the front of the witness box. Our attorney asked why counsel was approaching the witness (the witness had no testimony in relation to exhibits) and if he had no reason, would he return to his proper seat for questioning. The request was sustained and the attorney sheepishly returned to his table. This had a decided effect on his timing as well as his image before the jury.

Some jurisdictions allow free movement and some are very restrictive; this is important to know before the trial. If you are new to the jurisdiction, local counsel can be of tremendous assistance and may save you some embarrassment.

"Height power" should be used cautiously when speaking to the jury. The more closely you approach the jury, the greater your height power. Tall persons can momentarily startle jurors by quickly approaching the jury box.

In a personal injury case, the plaintiff's attorney, seated next to the jury, decided to stand during his questioning for voir dire. When the judge passed the jury to him he quickly stood up, and the two closest jurors were visibly startled. The closest juror remained very tense throughout the entire questioning process. Voir dire is usually best done from a seated position or a nonthreatening standing position.

For the normal exchange of communication, try to adjust your horizontal distance to eye level contact with the jury; however, if you back up too far, the increased distance will decrease the effectiveness of your interaction. If you must stand close to the jury box, tone down height advantage with nonthreatening, softer gestures and softer voice inflections. (Nonthreatening gestures are represented by open palm movements in the horizontal plane below your rib cage.)

How you use vertical space while standing telegraphs some fairly universal body language messages. Illustration (2.1c) is the image of a comfortable male. Deviations from the erect standing position as depicted in illustration (2.1d) will cost the slouched figure credibility points. A similar comparison for the seated position is represented by (2.1e) and (2.1f).

Height power can be controlled, to limited degrees, if the person is unusually short or tall. The shorter person can negate height power by getting the taller person to take a seated position. Most people when seated are at a similar eye level. If the short person stands while the taller person is still seated, the shorter person has gained height power. Vertical power can be increased or decreased to coincide with your objectives.

VERTICAL POSTURING

2.1c • Dominant Standing

2.1d • Submissive Standing

2.1e • Dominant Seated

2.1f • Submissive Seated

HORIZONTAL SPACE

Size power is the second major area of posturing, and it relates to the horizontal plane. In our society, size is a dominant, superior, or aggressive attribute. The more space you occupy, the more power you express. Compare illustrations (2.1g) and (2.1h), which visually demonstrate this basic principle of size power. Generally, you stand farther from high status people than from equal or low status people.

"Spreading yourself out" over a table or desk, with elbows out, can easily create an image of interrogation during an interview with a witness or client. The larger the image you present to another the more

HORIZONTAL POSTURING

2.1g
• Dominant
• Elbows Out
• More Space

2.1h
• Submissive
• Elbows In
• Less Space

authoritarian your demeanor. Conversely, shrinking your size power may create a greater sense of rapport between two people, as you now occupy a space similar to each other. Illustrations (2.1l) and (2.1j) demonstrate this difference.

When speaking to witnesses or jurors, if one or both hands are placed on your hips, thereby extending your horizontal space, you project aggressiveness or dominance. If you suddenly substantially increase your horizontal space, it is generally perceived as an aggressive act. The same can be said for sudden changes in the use of vertical space. The opposite is also true in both zones; if you give up space, the signal is more submissive.

A person who is ready to fight increases his control over the amount of space in both the vertical and horizontal planes. To balloon yourself out makes you appear more threatening. Rapid changes in body movement expansions in these two planes add additional emphasis to a show of power. During trials, depositions, and all forms of negotiation, you can greatly add or detract from your verbal messages by the use of positive or negative body language. Gaining power may be positive in some cases, but may work against you in others. The important thing is to decide upon the image you desire and to be complementary in your approach.

Lawyers

One of your goals is to convince the jury that you are knowledgeable and confident of your case. Correct posture can help you accomplish this goal.

Jurors

Watch how the jurors sit, stand, and walk in and out of the courtroom. Generally speaking, jurors who expand their vertical and horizontal space zones have more authoritative, confident, or aggressive personalities and tend to be the jury leaders.

HORIZONTAL POSTURING

2.1i
- Dominant
- Elbows Out
- More Space

2.1j
- Submissive
- Elbows In
- Less Space

BODY ANGLES

Body angles mirror psychological orientations and moods. Friendly body angles (2.2a) are those in which you are directly facing another person with an open front. Anything that closes off your frontal exposure detracts from friendliness. Folded arms, buttoned coats, vests, notebooks, charts, or other physical objects between you and the other person all act as blocking devices that can be translated into decreased friendliness. You can also use your body as a blocking device. Illustrations (2.2b) and (2.2c) rotate the model from a 45 degree angle to a 90 degree angle to demonstrate this effect.

On occasion you may speak to another person by turning just your head rather than your shoulders and body. The message being communicated is one of limited interest. You learn culturally that maximum interest requires full frontal exposure. Blocking devices indicate that you are either physically uncomfortable or are psychologically protecting yourself from unwanted communications or contacts. You do, of course, need to adjust your interpretations to specific situations. People may fold their arms because they are cold or tired or because they feel stress or are afraid. Thus, when trying to gain and maintain rapport with jurors, blocking signals normally should be avoided.

People who try to make body language assessments without considering the interactional effect of the individual parts (overall pattern) are greatly reducing their accuracy. It is like seeing one word in a sentence and trying to guess what the person wants to say. The more words we are able to read the more accurate our assessment of what the author wants to say.

BODY ANGLES

2.2a
• Open
• Parallel Hips
• Friendly

2.2b
• Partially Closed
• 45° Rotation
• Decreased Friendliness

2.2c
• Closed
• Perpendicular
• Unfriendly

Lawyers

Try to always directly face the jury during opening/closing statements and avoid facing sideways to the jury.

Jurors

If you are open and facing the jurors, watch to see who is open with you and who is closed. The jury's open response to your openness shows interest and rapport. The jury's closed response to your openness indicates a problem.

TENSION

Tension is one of your most important body language communicators. Tension is transferable. Nineteenth-century studies of crowd behavior referred to tension transference by names such as "social contagion." Tension can be transferred to one person or it can ripple through a crowd. An understanding of tension transference can be used to increase, decrease, or maintain a given tension state. You can increase tension among jurors, witnesses, or clients by using height and size power incorrectly. Tension can also be increased through unfriendly or power gestures or by using the body as a blocking device. Uncoordinated communication (when body language sends one set of signals and words send the opposite signals) also tends to generate tension.

Unpopular people, or people who cause others to withdraw from them, tend to communicate a high percentage of mixed signals. For example, we are often uncomfortable around new immigrants, strongly identified bilingual persons, or members of another cultural group. They give off signals that are appropriate for their own ethnic groups but use language associated with the dominant culture. Of course, the reverse is also found.

Many aspects of tension are similar to the body language indicators that we associate with lying behavior. When you are under tension there are changes in your internal body chemistry, muscle reactions, and ability to concentrate, as well as such obvious skin changes as facial flushing. When you are tense and stressed, you tend, both psychologically and physically, to feel uncomfortable. It is very difficult for the average person to significantly lie without some form of stress. As the severity of stress increases, so do the physiological changes in the body.

It is important that witnesses be relaxed before they testify; otherwise, you run the risk of jury members interpreting their stress signals as lying. I will discuss that in the next chapter but note here that tension and stress will tend to reduce witness credibility; people under stress have a more difficult time processing information, take longer to reply, and tend to speak more slowly.

During delivery of opening and closing statements, the elimination of body and voice tension is critical. Attorneys who are habitually nervous and transmit tense body language signals should practice breathing or muscle-relaxing exercises to reduce their tension. Remember, tension is transferable and you do not want a tense, uncomfortable jury.

Illustrations (2.3a), (2.3b), (2.3c), and (2.3d) demonstrate normal tension signals being communicated by witnesses, from least amount of tension to most amount of tension. In the first illustration, the hands and profile are open, thereby reflecting confidence. The clasped hands in (2.3b) and crossed arms across chest in (2.3c) are blocking devices and reflect less confidence than the first illustration. In (2.3d) the illustrated witness has blocked his body and face as though he were trying to hide.

The progressive amounts of tension expressed in the legs and feet is illustrated in (2.3e) through (2.3h). In a relaxed position legs are "open" and feet are resting comfortably on the floor. As tension increases people tend to pull their legs and feet toward their body centers; ankles are crossed, one ankle is put over a leg, and in the third stage one knee is crossed over the other (2.3f), (2.3g), and (2.3h). Preparing your witnesses to testify includes helping them to remain open and

HAND AND ARM TENSION

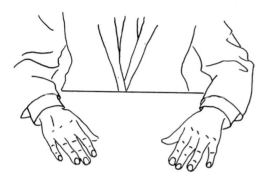

2.3a
- Open
- Relaxed

2.3b
- Clasped
- Some Tension

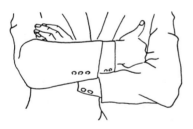

2.3c
- Arms Crossed
- More Tension

2.3d
- Arms Crossed
- Hands in Fists
- Hands Blocking Mouth
- Very Tense

FEET AND LEG TENSION

2.3e
• Open
• Relaxed

2.3f
• Ankles Crossed
• Some Tension

2.3g
• Ankle Crossed Over Knee
• More Tension

2.3h
• Knee Over Knee
• Angled Away
• Very Tense

relaxed so the jury does not misinterpret their signs of tension as lying behavior.

Lying behavior involves tension, but tension does not always involve lying behavior. Both lying and tension have the same signals but in different patterns. The differences are sometimes difficult for the average person to determine. This will be discussed in the section on lying behavior, but, basically, tension shows a slower rate of change than does lying behavior, which will change with the topic.

Lawyers

The more calm and relaxed you appear the more confidence the jury will have in you.

Jurors

Watch to see how tense and intimidated the jurors are. Leaders and strong personalities tend to feel in control at all times and thus feel less tense and less intimidated.

GESTURING

We use hand movements to accentuate a point, as well as to convey a psychological mood. For example, contrast a parent who is directly pointing a finger at a child she is scolding with one who is waving at her child with an open palm. The hand movements emphasize a point while at the same time conveying the psychological mood of the communicator. Gesturing is one of the most effective body language tools by which we can transfer an internal feeling to another person. We use hand gestures in two planes: the vertical and the horizontal. Within each of these two planes we have three basic hand positions: (a) palm toward the other person (2.4a), (b) back of the hand toward the other person (2.4b), and (c) side of the hand toward the other person (2.4c).

GESTURING HAND POSITIONS

2.4a
- Palming
- Friendly

2.4b
- Backhanding
- Unfriendly

2.4c
- Side of Hand
- Power

If your intent toward the other person is friendly, you subconsciously show them your palms. Waving at someone is a friendly example of "palming" them. Palming gestures elicit the same subconscious effect on someone as waving at them. How many witnesses have you seen take the courtroom oath of truth who didn't raise their right hands with their palms outward toward the clerk? They are told to raise their right hand but are given no instructions on hand positioning. The back of the hand is an unfriendly sign. Showing someone a fist is to give them the back of the hand. Obscene gesturing is typically done with backhanded positions. The side of the hand is used for aggression or emphasis and is a dramatic type of expression.

Gesturing in the upper plane, the area above the rib cage, carries more force and represents a more dominant movement than lower plane gesturing. Compare (2.4d) and (2.4e). Now compare the three hand positions in (2.4f), (2.4g), and (2.4h). The message communicated by illustration (2.4g) is one of aggression. The model in this illustration has a partially closed fist with pointed finger in the upper vertical plane.

Although the lower horizontal plane is less dominant and aggressive (2.4i), it still can be used when portraying aggression (2.4j) and unfriendliness (2.4k) by changing hand positions. Body language is culturally learned and subconsciously controlled, so that people are constantly giving away their inner feelings through gesturing and other physical actions. People who do not like you tend to increase the frequency with which they show you the backs of their hands. Someone attempting to dominate another will use the side of his hand more often while gesturing.

Speed of gesturing is also important, and in combination with the vertical and horizontal planes, increases the intended emphasis. Fast-paced gestures in the upper plane are aggressive, while open, slow-paced gestures in the lower plane are friendly. Gestures directed to the sides of others are friendlier than those directed straight toward them.

Gesturing is very important during opening and closing statements when speaking to the jury. Throughout the majority of your speech you will want to palm the jury. To emphasize a point, you can use side-of-

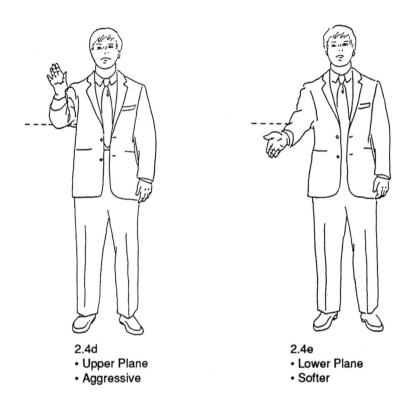

2.4d
• Upper Plane
• Aggressive

2.4e
• Lower Plane
• Softer

hand gestures, but you do not want to appear threatening and therefore need to slow down the gestures. Pointing directly at the jury can make you appear accusatory or convey the impression of a teacher who is lecturing. In practice you will want to use a combination of gestures. In order to sensitize yourself to the moods of others, it is helpful to observe changes in their gesturing patterns. This point is particularly meaningful when you are attempting to observe lying behavior.

The important thing to remember about gesturing is that it shows the amount of psychological involvement people have while talking. The more involved they are the more gesturing they will display. The more

GESTURING UPPER PLANE

2.4f
• Palm
• Friendly

2.4g
• Side
• Power

2.4h
• Backhanded
• Unfriendly

GESTURING LOWER PLANE

2.4i
• Palming
• Friendly

2.4j
• Side
• Emphasis

2.4k
• Backhanded
• Unfriendly

feeling and involvement you have in what you are saying the more you subconsciously gesture to get the other people involved in your speech or in order to convince them of your position.

Lawyers

Gesturing during your speech (without crossing over to the aggressive extreme) will increase your chances of generating more interest and involvement on the part of the jury.

Jurors

Gesturing shows emotion and involvement. Watch when a juror's gesturing increases and decreases. As a general rule, jurors who are good for the plaintiff show a lot of gesturing, and defense jurors gesture very little. Jurors who are very animated generally get emotionally involved in a subject very quickly.

EYE CONTACT

Sustained eye contact in our society normally creates tension, stress, and anxiety. In normal conversations we maintain eye contact about 50 percent of the time while we are speaking and about 80 percent of the time when we are listening. A higher or lower degree of eye contact represents a change in your psychological position, degree of dominance, or the desired amount of interaction.

If you are attempting to dominate another, you will maintain eye contact 100 percent of the time. Throughout recorded history, averted eyes have been used in a large percentage of world cultures to represent submission. Nearly continuous eye contact can also mean infatuation and is readily observed between "lovers" (and is the one exception to the stress rule).

In the courtroom setting, the total amount of eye contact is increased because you are continuously evaluating others and they are evaluating you. If your goal is to make another person uncomfortable, sustained eye contact will have that effect. If you want witnesses or others to be comfortable, you must stay within our cultural norms. Sustained eye contact psychologically tends to affect other people by raising their respiration rates and blood pressures. Staring does create physical discomfort.

Opening and closing statements before the jury require eye contact with each juror. Eye contact increases the amount of confidence that jury members feel toward you and permits you to assess more carefully their reactions. While before the jury, you will want to identify the foreperson as early as possible and increase your eye contact with him or her. Eye contact is especially important during voir dire, and I will say more about that later.

It has been said that eyes are the windows to a person's soul. At a minimum, eyes tell you a great deal about the internal moods and psychological states of others. When you like things, your pupils dilate; when you dislike things, your pupils contract. You also look at objects longer if you like them than if you dislike them. Advertisers have used these concepts for years.

Eye movements generally represent a direct link to brain functioning, which is associated with left and right directional eye gaze. People generally look to their upper right when they are thinking about what they are going to say or when they are thinking about an answer. In other words, cognitive association is usually accompanied by a gaze to the upper right. You look to your lower right when you respond to questions about your feelings. Eye movements to your upper right are used when you access your memories for stored information. You look to your lower left when you talk to yourself. Basically, right gazing is observed when the person is searching for memory items and left gazing if the person is offering an opinion. If these two eye signals are reversed, the person may be trying to manipulate you. If you ask a witness questions requiring memory (for example, what time of day her accident occurred) and she looks to the right (normal thinking mode), you would probably continue to cross-examine and see if her pattern continues. If the pattern of gazing to the right continues, you can

Chart III

EYE MOVEMENT POSITIONS OF A SPEAKER

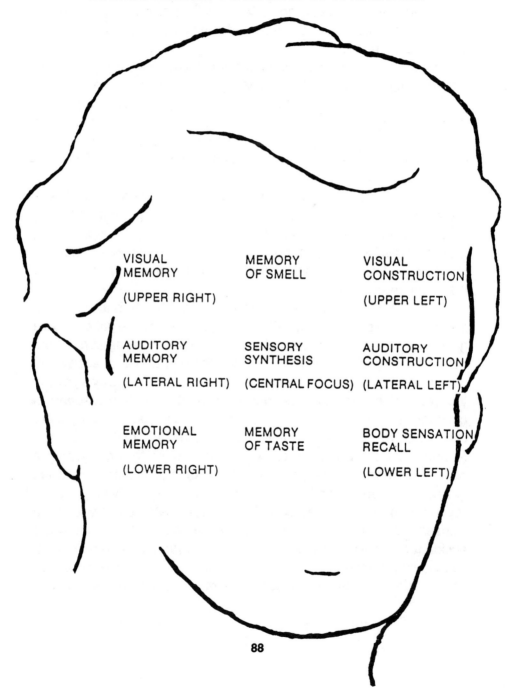

VISUAL
MEMORY

(UPPER RIGHT)

MEMORY
OF SMELL

VISUAL
CONSTRUCTION

(UPPER LEFT)

AUDITORY
MEMORY

SENSORY
SYNTHESIS

AUDITORY
CONSTRUCTION

(LATERAL RIGHT)

(CENTRAL FOCUS)

(LATERAL LEFT)

EMOTIONAL
MEMORY

MEMORY
OF TASTE

BODY SENSATION
RECALL

(LOWER RIGHT)

(LOWER LEFT)

accurately tell when she remembers something. If she is putting together an answer on the spur of the moment, the right gazing pattern would change to a left gazing pattern. I recommend that you practice observing this phenomena casually until your ability to read eye signals comes "naturally." Human behavior is rarely absolute; therefore, it needs to be assessed in its entirety. Always pay more attention to the pattern than to one particular movement or action.

When a person's body language is giving off signals of discomfort, you have exceeded his individual level of tolerance. In fact, with regard to witnesses you should consistently compare their verbal and visual signals for differences. If the two signals differ, the body language is a more accurate picture because it is usually controlled subconsciously. Being able to consciously change all of your nonverbal messages to fool someone becomes increasingly difficult as the other person's ability to understand body language increases. Once you become sophisticated in interpreting body language movements, you can often spot an attempted cover-up within a few seconds. As an example, I was able to assist in solving a large robbery case after speaking with the alleged "victim" for several minutes. He later admitted to having set up the entire event and the police recovered the money. Body language assessment is a visual polygraph test.

Lawyers

Maintaining eye contact with the jurors is very important because it shows them you are confident in what you are doing and gives you the opportunity to assess their reactions.

Jurors

Looking at someone indicates liking or interest. Generally, the more eye contact the jury has with you the better your case is going.

LYING BEHAVIOR

I have reserved my discussion about lying behavior for the latter part of this chapter because it requires the observer to be knowledgeable of another person's total body language movements. A basic generalization to keep in mind is that people are "open" when they are telling the truth and "closed" when they are lying. When you are relaxed and confident your body language is open, including arms, hands, legs, feet, and body angles. When you are stressful or when you are lying, you tend to bring your body into your imaginary centers much like a ball. And when you do extend yourself, it will be for shorter distances than your usual gestures and movements.

When people lie they use half-gestures and extend their arms or hands only partially, as though trying not to overextend themselves. Gesturing frequency also decreases when a person is lying, and the speed of gesturing is altered. Lying people may gesture more quickly, as though they are trying to make a point and get it out of the way, or people will gesture more slowly, as if they are unsure of themselves.

People also bring their hands to their faces, mouths, or hair when they are lying or are unsure of themselves (they psychologically cover up their words). Increased preening is often a sign of uneasiness. Crossing of feet at the knees or ankles is also a sign of "closing down." Crossing your ankles underneath your chair is a greater sign of stress than crossing them in front of your chair. Note that women normally cross their ankles more than men.

To observe the cumulative effects of stress, follow illustrations (2.5a) through (2.5g). The illustrated model goes from an open position in both the upper and lower body sections to a closed position in (2.5g). The progression provides the following sequence of indicators: (a) (2.5a) shows an open front, legs, hands, relaxed face, and parallel body angles; (b) in (2.5b) the model begins to close up; feet cross at the ankle, fingers clench the chair, and the facial muscles begin to tighten; (c) by illustration (2.5c) the legs remain crossed and are pulled under the chair with knees pulled together. Women frequently use the crossed-ankle, legs-under-the-chair position; therefore, it is a more natural movement for them and should be interpreted differently than for men. In all cases, remember that it is the pattern that is important and that the male/female patterns differ slightly; (d) in (2.5d) the arms are used as blocking devices and the clenched hands indicate a fighting response; (e) figure (2.5e) has reverted to using crossed legs as a blocking device; (f) turning to the side physically and psychologically provides a larger shield for one's body organs (2.5f); (g) finally in (2.5g) the person has lowered his upper body toward his center in a ball-like position to minimize total exposure and has covered his mouth with his hand.

The sequence of actions represented by the lying behavior illustrations will vary with circumstance, gender, and individual physical differences. Watching the witness's or subject's body language signs over time will, however, provide much additional information.

It is also important to differentiate between normal stress and stress that is associated with lying. When a juror first comes into the courtroom, it is common to observe numerous stress signs. As that person becomes acclimated to the courtroom, he will gradually relax. It is this pattern that we associate with normal stress.

When individuals lie, they will tend to go through a series of open-to-closed, closed-to-open body language movements. Additionally, lying behavior triggers body reactions that are similar to embarrassment; body chemistry changes. Changed body chemistry can create a dry mouth accompanied by lip licking, perspiring, heavy breathing, facial discoloration, stomach noises, general nervous twitching, hand-to-face movements, and increased preening. Individuals generally decrease the amount of eye contact when they lie. Furthermore, they will also glance downward more frequently.

If facial expressions change very little, the person may have extraordinary control. This is frequently the case with people who are habitual liars or who have psychopathic personalities. Most accomplished liars, however, even though they have excellent control of their facial expressions, do not have similar control over other aspects of body language. Most people are good at "masking" their facial expressions—they learn to smile when they're not happy and cry when they're

LYING BEHAVIOR STRESS SEQUENCE

2.5a
• Open

2.5b
• Ankles Crossed

2.5c
• Ankles Crossed Underneath
• Hands in Fists
• Knees Together

LYING BEHAVIOR STRESS SEQUENCE

2.5d
- Ankles Crossed Underneath
- Hands in Fists
- Knees Together
- Arms Crossed Over Chest

2.5e
- Ankles Crossed Over Knee
- Arms Crossed On Chest

2.5f
- Knee Crossed Over Knee
- Body Angled 45°
- Arms Crossed Over Chest

2.5g
- Knee Crossed Over Knee
- Body Angled Perpendicular
- Hand Covering Face

not sad. I pay little attention to facial expressions when I evaluate a person's body language.

Other facial movements indicating stress include nose touching, hand to cheek, body shifting, feet shuffling, foot tapping, and other similar "nervous" behaviors. Playing with pens, keys, jewelry, or hair also releases tension. People tend to be least aware of their hands and feet, so watch those areas carefully. Hands are often the best indicators of tension and are usually the easiest to read.

The plaintiff in one of my cases bit his lip whenever he was uncomfortable with a question. When you become sensitive to body language, similar clues can be quickly used to your advantage.

When examining or cross-examining a witness, signs of stress provide extensive clues about lying and areas that the witness is trying to hide or has uncomfortable feelings about.

TWO KINDS OF LIES

There are two ways to lie: (1) **concealment**—withholding information by being silent; and (2) **falsification**—giving out false information as a cover-up.

Concealment is the easiest way to lie because it causes less psychological stress in the individual lying. The lying person blanks out the question and just "forgets" to volunteer the truth. This happens quite often in group situations in which the person can remain anonymous in the group. Knowing this, you can elicit much more truthful information by asking positive questions that are aimed at the jury as a group than you can by asking negative questions that are aimed at individuals.

For instance, if you ask a jury panel a negative question such as "How many of you could not award two million dollars under any circumstances?" and nobody raises a hand, you have no idea how many people are concealing their true feelings. But if you ask the group a positive question such as "How many of you could award a person two million dollars if the case justified that large an award?" you will see more accurately who has trouble with big awards, and, more importantly, you have forced the prospective jurors to physically respond. People who could never award two million dollars regardless of the real damages will do one of two things: (a) they will raise their hands to join the crowd (falsification); or (b) they will not raise their hands, in which case your question has accomplished its goal. The people who could not award two million dollars but raised their hands anyway (falsifying their feelings) have publicly declared themselves and therefore have taken the first step towards being persuaded to question their true feelings.

Falsification is the most difficult way to lie and causes the most internal turmoil. It is therefore easier to detect and is also recorded in the transcript. For instance, in the Oliver North case it was discovered after the verdict that three seated jurors directly lied during voir dire on very important issues.

The two most important things to remember about lying behavior in the courtroom are (1) if an issue is very important to your case, try to get each juror to respond individually to your question; and (2) if you suspect jurors or witnesses are going to lie about an issue, make it psychologically more stressful for them to do so.

THREE BASIC LYING EMOTIONS

People exhibit any or all of three basic emotions when they lie: (1) **apprehension** (most people have negative stressful feelings if they believe their lies will be detected); (2) **guilt** (most people have negative stressful feelings associated with a guilty conscience when they know they have to live with their lies); and (3) **duping** (some people have positive happy feelings knowing they are deceiving someone. You have to recognize their motives and make sure their responses are well documented).

The important thing to remember is that two of the lying emotions are negative and create internal stress, but one of the lying emotions (duping) is positive and will not cause internal stress. Because they possess this positive lying emotion some people are perfectly calm when they deceive others and may completely pass a polygraph test. Most jurors and witnesses, however, are not seasoned "con men" and therefore will give out the stressful signals when lying.

INCREASING LIARS' STRESS

You want to increase the stress of people you suspect of lying so (1) they will change their minds and obtain relief by telling you the truth, or (2) if they continue to lie both you and others will be able to detect the deceit. You can increase the apprehensive stress of lying people by showing them you are suspicious, convincing them that you will catch them in a lie and telling them the consequences of their lies, and making them think that the stakes are too high for them to continue lying. You can increase the guilty stress of lying people by reinforcing the notion that they have to live with their lies, convincing them to tell the truth in the interests of fair play, showing them how lying violates social norms, emphasizing the seriousness of lying, and giving them a way out.

Lawyers

Stress and lying exhibit the same signals but show slightly different patterns or combinations. Any tension or stress signals you give out may be wrongly interpreted by the jury as lying behavior. If the jury thinks you are lying to them, it will be a major blow to your case from which it will be very difficult to recover. Eliminate as much of your tension as possible. Remember, tension is self-induced. You are what you think you are. If you think fearful thoughts you will become tense. If you think happy thoughts you will become relaxed.

Jurors

Statistics show that one out of every five jurors lies during voir dire. You want to be able to evaluate the truthfulness of every juror's answers. Would you trust someone who lied to you at the beginning of the trial to be fair at the end of the trial?

WITNESS DEMEANOR

You will want to increase your witnesses' images as open, honest, and credible people. Consequently, you don't want them to exhibit signs of stress that may be interpreted as lying behavior. In (2.6a) the witness is in an open, alert position. As you progressively move through (2.6b), (2.6c), and (2.6d), the model becomes tense, closed in, and appears in (2.6d) to be hiding something. Stress body language has too many similarities to lying behavior to leave this set of variables to chance.

Attorneys may wish to practice proper demeanor with witnesses or provide them with copies of these illustrations. It is unfortunate to have the jury wrongfully discredit testimony because the witness appears to be lying or withholding information. You may choose to remind the witnesses to copy your open, alert demeanor when you are seated at your table. It takes more effort on your part, but the impression for the jury is usually worth the effort. It also forces you into good habits that can benefit you throughout your career.

UPPER- AND LOWER-CLASS BODY LANGUAGE

The personal image that represents authority and credibility in America is basically the image of the socially educated upper middle class. "Upper-middle-class" people appear to others to be in control, portray erect posture, and possess a generally confident demeanor. The more you deviate from this image the greater your loss of credibility. Illustration (2.7a) shows the proper demeanor in the seated position. Illustration (2.7b) portrays the male upper-middle-class relaxed position. If you become much "sloppier" than this, you lose credibility as a socially educated/cultured/confident person.

Lower-class demeanor is just as stereotyped. Illustration (2.7c) depicts a lower-class male seating position. Feet are not flat on the floor, legs and arms are protruding into adjacent spaces, and the person is slouched forward. In (2.7d) the increased sprawl even more

WITNESS DEMEANOR

2.6a
- Open
- Confident

2.6b
- Open with Clasped Hands
- Controlled Tension
- Credible

2.6c
- Partially Closed
- Stressful
- Some Credibility Loss
- Defensive

2.6d
- Closed
- Angled Away
- Hands in Fist
- Hands Covering Mouth
- Not Credible

2.7a
• Involved
• Alert

2.7b
• Relaxing
• Controlled

strongly states nonverbally that he either is a person who lacks self-discipline or is uncaring and insensitive to social norms.

Other characteristics normally associated with the lower class are a drooping chin, slouched shoulders, a rolling walk, and jerky, unsure gesturing. With a combination of lower-class body language, sloppy dress, and poor speech patterns, it is hard to gain credibility either as a professional person or as a witness.

LOWER-CLASS BODY LANGUAGE

2.7c
• Involved
• Uncontrolled

2.7d
• Relaxing
• Undisciplined

The important thing to remember about body language is that there are cultural, gender, and motivational differences among jurors. It is therefore very important to know as much about the total person as possible in order to accurately assess the combination of clues rather than a few individual clues.

SPACE

In chapter 1 you were briefly introduced to the concepts of social and territorial space. Each person has four basic horizontal zones of social space that have psychological importance—intimate, personal, social, and public. You can consciously use these zones with juries and witnesses to create numerous reactions. Illustration (2.8a) shows the intimate zone (one foot or closer). You allow only your closest friends into this zone: your wife, husband, children, or lovers. At a distance of one to three feet, you have the personal zone, close enough to allow other people to place their hands on your shoulders (2.8b). You feel comfortable touching those "allowed" in this zone, but you are not comfortable hugging or kissing them. This zone is usually used by very good friends.

The social zone starts at approximately three to four feet away from you. This is a comfortable distance at which to shake hands, converse with coworkers, or sit across the table at lunch. Illustration (2.8c) indicates that social distance is just close enough to touch at arm's length. This zone is used by acquaintances.

The public zone, over four feet from you, is reserved for strangers (2.8d). Social intercourse on a public street between strangers requires this distance unless space does not permit it. For example, in the elevator you are often forced into another's personal or intimate zone; you compensate by pretending the other people are not there or react to them as if they were nonpersons.

When you enter others' spatial zones without welcome, you tend to increase their stress levels. As others become familiar with you and you establish rapport, you can gradually move into their social or even their personal zones. The closer you can approach another person without being threatening the better your rapport, the more positive interaction you will receive from them, and the stronger your interaction will be. When people are close and comfortable, they normally have a higher concentration level and a better relationship.

Your initial contact with juries and witnesses should include the conscious use of space (2.9a) and (2.9b). After rapport has been estab-

HORIZONTAL SPACE ZONES

2.8a
• Intimate

2.8b
• Personal

2.8c
• Social

2.8d
• Public

lished with a witness or the jury, you can enhance greater intimacy through the conscious use of spatial zones. Opening and closing statements therefore require different sensitivity to space.

An opening statement requires that you remain at a greater distance than during a closing statement. In an opening statement you and the jury are virtually strangers. Because the courtroom is a formal setting and you and the jurors are strangers, I recommend you stand at least six to eight feet away from the jury. In a closing argument I recommend that you start at least eight feet away from the jury and gradually move in as close as you can without making the jury uncomfortable. A gauge of how well you relate to the jury is how close they will psychologically allow you to approach them before they become uncomfortable. As you approach the jury and they show signs of stress, you should retreat. The greater your rapport with jury members the closer they can be approached without showing discomfort. Height power and directional gestures become increasingly important as you approach another's personal zone.

In our culture women can approach both males and females more closely than can men. Consequently, it is usually easier for women to gain rapport than it is for men, but for the same reason it is harder for them to gain power. Nevertheless, when jury members begin to cross their arms and legs, lean backwards, or turn to the side you may be violating their space bubble.

Social space zones vary for different cultural groups, as they vary for males and females. People from the Near East who are strangers are often comfortable within either the social or the personal zones. Women use less distance with each other than they do with men. Women talking to other women professionally can narrow social distances by one complete zone and be comfortable. Women approaching men professionally can shade half a zone off the male normative distance and be relatively safe.

You do not need to memorize a dictionary of spatial differences for every subgroup because by watching people's body language and remembering the four zones, you can tell when they are becoming uncomfortable. Maintaining awareness is the key to interpersonal intercourse.

Territorial space is the permanent space you feel you own or have a right to control. Examples of territorial space are your homes, your offices, jury boxes, or your chairs. The closer others come to the center of your territorial space the stronger is your physical or psychological response: the same principle as social space. The longer you occupy a given physical space the stronger your sense of ownership. Jurors have boundaries around their jury box and a strong sense of social bonding generated by their common task. Their new identity is nearly instant and psychologically becomes stronger as the trial progresses. The longer the trial the stronger their territorial feelings of "owning" their part of the jury box.

In terms of statuses and roles, you have a basic understanding regarding social and territorial space. In terms of dominance, the laws are:

(1) Dominants control more territory
(2) Dominants are freer to move about
(3) Dominants are accorded greater bodily space
(4) Subordinates yield space to dominants when meeting
(5) Dominants control more of the desired or preferred space

Different space usage is a matter of class, status, and ethnic differences. Space also has an inverse relationship to liking; the more you like someone, the nearer you allow the person. The more space a person controls, the more dominant he becomes; dominant people project a larger "space bubble."

Femininity has been partially judged by how little space is taken up; masculinity is judged by expansiveness. Even though women traditionally take up less space than men, theirs is more frequently violated; both sexes approach women more closely than they do men.

JURY AND WITNESS SPACE

2.9a
• Decreased Stress

2.9b
• Increased Stress

COURTROOM SPACE ZONES

There are many space zones in every courtroom: the judge's space, the witnesses' space, the jury box, the lawyers' tables.

Lawyers

As you move around the courtroom you are constantly going in and out of different space zones. How you use space between you and other people can be a real advantage for you when you are presenting your case.

Jurors

The longer the jurors sit on a case the stronger their ownership feeling is for the jury box. Treat their area with respect and be aware of how they react when you approach them.

TIME

In chapter 1 I covered some fundamental aspects of time usage in the courtroom regarding recesses, time of day, and length of interaction. The scheduling of witnesses should take into consideration the principles of recency and primacy. In a sequential episode of events, we are most influenced by those episodes that either come first or last and are less influenced by episodes that occur in the middle. Consequently, poor witnesses will be noticed least in a "middle" position if all other factors are equal. Effective use of time, then, requires consideration of the following points:

(1) The effect that time of day will have on juror comprehension and state of alertness. Alertness is maximum between 9:30 and 11:30 a.m. and 2:00 to 4:00 p.m.

(2) The use of recency and primacy principles when scheduling primary and secondary witnesses (good witnesses first and last).

(3) Psychological timing ploys to rattle your opponents and force them to interrupt their smoothness.

(4) Use of the seventeen-to-twenty-minute rule to maintain a high degree of attention and concentration.

(5) The use of macro time planning to more effectively control the entire courtroom "drama."

Different time factors play a very important part in every good attorney's overall strategy.

FOUR MAIN TIMING CONSIDERATIONS

1. How long should you take for voir dire? Assuming the judge has given you some flexibility in voir dire, try to use as much time as you can getting to know the jury panel. As long as you are organized, know what you want, and are working directly toward a goal, you will be able to build rapport with the jury. If you are disorganized and unfocused, the judge probably will cut you off, but just as importantly the jury will form a negative first impression and psychologically will cut you off.

2. How long should you take for opening/closing statements? In most cases thirty minutes or less is enough time if you concentrate on the right points. In some special cases you may want to make a longer opening or closing statement. An example of a legitimate longer opening statement is if you want the jury to focus on you during the trial rather than on other parts of your case. Some skillful trial attorneys want to be the source of the trial information and so they spend a great deal of time communicating all of the facts and conclusions to the jury. This strategy must be handled very adroitly because it can very easily backfire.

3. How long should you take for direct/cross-examinations? The most important thing to decide is what you want out of each witness. Organize your questions to get what you want as quickly as possible and then stop. The longer you go on the more you tax the jury's attention span and the more you may water down your cross-examination.

4. What should be your order of witnesses? The longer the plaintiff/prosecutor's case goes without a problem witness the better it is for the plaintiff/prosecutor. In most cases you want to schedule hostile or adverse witnesses later in the trial. Some plaintiff's attorneys like to surprise the defendants or hope to catch them unprepared or want to lock up their testimony by calling hostile or adverse witnesses to testify first. This may work beautifully in some cases, but be very careful because it has the potential to backfire on you. The last witnesses should be as trouble-free as possible in order to leave the jury with positive feelings.

Lawyers

The timing of your case, the overall flow of your evidence, and the attention span of your jury are very important issues involved in the effectiveness of your presentation. Understanding and using these issues to your advantage will keep your jury interested and enhance your credibility.

Jurors

The jurors' attention spans are typically very short because the jurors are less involved in the case than the participants. In order to keep the jurors interested you must make the trial interesting, moving, and understandable.

VERBAL IMAGE

While people are speaking you assess their verbal skills and conceptual levels of conversation. Middle-class language patterns, preferably patterned after the jurors' own locale, will carry more credibility than language patterns that contain poor grammar, mispronounced words, or slang. Attorneys who assist the jury by clarifying definitions and technical terminology increase personal credibility with the jury. Positive rapport is gained by providing explanations, by using courtesy statements that clarify procedure or expectations, and by treating listeners as intellectual equals.

The legal environment focuses on words and their exact translations. Communication between two lawyers typically concentrates on spoken and written words and assumes that both lawyers understand each other. Research has shown that lay people put approximately 10 percent of their focus on actual words spoken. Most lay people concentrate the majority of their attention on how words are presented to determine what has been communicated. Jury trials could be handled very differently if your jury were made up of all lawyers. Words are very important, but how they are presented is also very important.

It is your job to explain an unfamiliar story in an unfamiliar setting to lay people in understandable terms. Remember, brilliance is the ability to make things simple. You must evaluate your jurors and educate them in a learnable manner. Most jurors, as a group, are very intelligent. They are just unfamiliar with the new setting and the new problems of the case. Waitresses, farmers, salespeople, and accountants know a lot about their work, but they typically know very little about medical malpractice lawsuits.

Vocabulary is an indication of education (university of "hard knocks") or motive (for example, cursing could indicate shock, anger, or fear) or both. If you listen to people speak you can discover a variety of clues about their personalities, including how they listen. For instance, some people listen and understand better if something is told to them in visual terms so that they can see a picture of it in their minds. They tend to express their ideas in visual terms, which is a mirror image of their listening channels.

VERBAL FEEDBACK

COMMUNICATE ON THEIR CHANNEL

VISUAL — I see, I look, I imagine, I view, I'm hazy, looking back, cast some light

KINESTHETIC — I feel, I can grasp, I can handle it

AUDITORY — I hear, it sounds, I can tune in, that tells me, I try to listen, that rings a bell

VERBAL CLUES

EMOTIONAL CLUES (Blue/Yellow)

I see	I feel	I can imagine
That look	I have a feeling	I view

TECHNICAL CLUES (Red/Green)

I think	I believe	I recall
I remember	I suspect	I calculate

Lawyers

Tell the jurors the story in an understandable, interesting manner so that they want to listen and become involved.

Jurors

Jurors' attention spans and understanding generally go hand in hand. As understanding goes up their attention spans increase. As understanding goes down their attention spans decrease.

Jurors are in one of three learning modes: (1) positive mode: learning and involved; (2) neutral mode: just sitting there pretending to pay attention; or (3) negative mode: becoming angry and frustrated. The more confused the jurors become the easier it is for them to fall into the neutral or negative mode.

SUMMARY

Visual communication is a very important part of the total information jurors use in order to reach their verdict. The majority of jury decisions are strongly shaded by emotions and are not decided simply by reasoning. In this sense, they are people first and jurors second. Their initial impressions of counsel, clients, and witnesses are long lasting and weigh heavily in the balance of trial outcomes.

As individuals, jurors like to help people they feel good about and find it difficult to be generous with individuals of whom they have negative impressions. Increasing your sensitivity to the most appropriate combination of dress, body language, space, time, and verbal image significantly increase your credibility and rapport with the jury.

During interpersonal interactions we constantly assess each other in five basic areas: appearance, demeanor, space usage, time usage, and verbalization. Four of these areas (appearance, demeanor, space usage, and time usage) constitute your nonverbal image. The fifth area (speech) is your verbal image. In order to help eliminate misinterpretations, you must be certain that your nonverbal image (the manner in which you say something) and your verbal image (what you say) are consistent with each other.

Normally your nonverbal messages are subconsciously controlled, while your verbal messages are consciously controlled. By consciously understanding and adjusting your nonverbal messages to fit your objective, you are improving your communication skills. As you consciously assess the nonverbal messages given out by your witnesses and jurors, you are better able to understand and react to them.

Your objectives in improving your interpersonal communication skills are to project a verbal and nonverbal image that will enhance your position and to have the knowledge and flexibility that allow you to react to your witnesses' and jurors' verbal and nonverbal messages.

Chapter 3 will cover case strategies and trial preparation of clients, witnesses and evidence.

PRETRIAL PREPARATION

INTRODUCTION

This chapter combines my courtroom experience with proven social science communication principles to design a workable case preparation system. The chapter shows how you can combine the social and the legal parts of your case in order to enhance your presentation to the jury. This system will assist you in organizing and maintaining a consistent strategy throughout the trial. This system is not by any means the only way to organize every case, but it works very well for any civil or criminal case.

CASE OUTLINE

Discovery is over, you have collected all of your evidence, and you are now preparing to go to trial. All of the pieces of the case must now be organized into a tightly scripted presentation that the jury will understand, become involved in, and believe in.

The twelve major areas discussed in this chapter are

1. Client information
2. Legal elements of the case
3. Expected jury instructions
4. Your case vs. your opponent's case
5. Ideal juror
6. Unwanted juror
7. Main points—opening and closing statements
8. Evidence to be introduced
9. Damages
10. Verdict desired
11. Judge or jury
12. Trial preparation outline

CLIENT INFORMATION

It is important to know all you can about your client because an important part of jury selection is whether or not jurors can identify with your client. It is also vital to keep in mind any problems your client may have, prior convictions, mental capacity, noticeable speech problems, unattractive image and demeanor, social or economic class, and health problems. Each individual problem of the client must be taken into consideration when working towards jury identification. Do you want your client

- (a) at your table
- (b) in the spectator section
- (c) sitting through the entire trial
- (d) leaving after his or her testimony
- (e) to have his or her family or friends present

Each of these situations may be beneficial in some cases and detrimental in others, which is why they must be considered in every case.

If your client is a corporation you still want to find out everything you can about it, including its reputation in the community and any good or bad media coverage about the case or any other incidents. If your client is a corporation you need to "humanize" it by stressing its people and how they benefit the community by increasing jobs, the economy, and so on. If you are opposing a corporation you want to present the corporation as a profit-driven machine. In addition to your own client you want to know everything about your adversaries.

ELEMENTS

Obviously the legal points to be proven are essential to highlight in the beginning. If a case legally is not complete and the judge directs the case out, it does not matter if the jury was on your side: the case is over.

JURY INSTRUCTION INTERROGATORIES

Discussing the probable instructions the jury will receive will assist in your choice of key words and phrases to be used during your case presentation. Another reason you want to evaluate the interrogatories to the jury in the beginning is because these are the ultimate questions the jury has to answer. Knowing the answers you need gives you some help in understanding who can ultimately agree with your answers.

CASE IN CHIEF—YOURS VS. OPPONENT'S

Charting your strengths and weaknesses against those of your adversaries keeps the different strategies as clear as possible. The strengths of your case may not necessarily be the weaknesses of your opponent's case, but they frequently will be the same. You know where you are coming from, but you need to know (if you don't already through pleadings and discovery) where your adversary is coming from and the focus of his case. Writing down the strengths and weaknesses of each side helps you develop strategies and gives you a checklist of points to be covered.

JUROR PROFILE—WHAT YOU WANT

You want the ideal juror profile to be a distillation of socio-psychological variables: a combination of the workable parts of different social science models that have been used in the past. This gives you an idea of whom, ideally, you would want on the jury. This check sheet also is used after the jury has been impaneled. Each juror is evaluated by the use of this list in order to understand the makeup of your final jury panel.

In the trial preparation outline at the end of this chapter, answering A through O under "Profile of the Ideal Juror" will give you your ideal juror. Obviously, you will not end up with many jurors who completely fit this profile. Your goal is to find jurors who are as close to this profile as you can within the venire.

JUROR PROFILE—WHAT YOU DON'T WANT

This is the most critical section as far as selecting the jury. At the top of the list should be the factor you have decided would be most damaging to your cause; other damaging factors are listed in descending order. In certain cases gender is extremely important, in other cases it is neutral. The same can be said for age, emotional and psychological models, status, occupation, and other factors. After listing undesirable factors, you can decide which jurors will be most damaging to your case.

In most cases lawyers spend their time looking for the wrong clues during voir dire. Instead of looking for your best jurors your focus should be on who are the most damaging people for your case and how you can remove them from the jury.

MAIN POINTS OF OPENING AND CLOSING STATEMENTS

The main points should be the same in both opening and closing statements and should coincide with the elements and the special interrogatories. Even the most complicated cases should be boiled down to three or four main points that you want the jury to be convinced of when they deliberate. Opening and closing statements can be effectively presented in a relatively short time if they are organized around your three or four main points.

EVIDENCE

You need to be acutely aware of how to best present all of the direct evidence and what demonstrative evidence can assist your case. Trial is like a puzzle: the outcome depends on how you put the pieces together.

DAMAGES

Plan how the damages are going to be presented, the amount of the anticipated awards, and how to covertly inflate or deflate emotions about these awards. Emotional involvement has a great deal of influence on both civil and criminal verdicts. Emotion in civil cases centers around empathy, sympathy, and fairness. Emotion in criminal cases centers around revenge, fear, punishment, and compassion. After you understand your case you will know which emotions will help you the most and which emotions will hurt you the most. You then gear your case to involve the jury's emotions for your benefit.

TYPE OF VERDICT DESIRED

Before you request a jury trial in a criminal case, know whether you want an acquittal, a finding of guilty, a verdict to a lesser crime, or a hung jury. Only about 26 percent of hung jury cases are ever retried. They are usually dropped, plea bargained, or in some other way fall through the cracks of the system.

In civil cases, voir dire basically will focus on the selection of either (a) an emotional or technical, or (b) a generous or tight-pocketed jury. Obviously, jury selection will depend upon whether your relationship is with the plaintiff or the defendant. In criminal cases voir dire is basically focused on (a) establishment or anti-establishment, or (b) conservative or liberal. Criminal juries are much easier to strike because of the greater differences in personalities that each side wants. Civil juries involve more personality traits, and both sides end up with a more blended ideal juror.

JUDGE OR JURY

Before the decision is made whether to try a case before a judge or jury, all the pluses and minuses of both your case and your opposition's case should be weighed. You will be able to see clearly and reinforce mentally the strengths and weaknesses of your case as well as those of your opposition. Following this procedure also helps organize ideas for opening and closing statements.

Communication, both verbal and nonverbal, is most effective when it is consistent and well organized throughout the entire trial. The visual impression of your client, you, and the witnesses must be included in your decision to select a particular trial strategy. In fact, the five basic areas of "personal assessment" listed in chapter 1 should be considered along with the legal strategy.

We know that in civil cases plaintiffs who are professionals recover less from juries than from judges. The critical element is the capacity of jurors to identify with the plaintiff. Jurors are typically of a lower social status than professionals and tend to feel that professionals are already well off. For example, recovery for plaintiffs in general is about 61 percent, while professionals as a group recover 50 percent or less (with the exception of engineers who have a recovery rate of 67 percent). Generally, plaintiffs in civil cases who have a strong emotional appeal are best tried before juries; nonemotional, long, technical cases will generally provide a better outcome for the plaintiff if they are tried before a judge. The defense would want to reverse this strategy.

In criminal cases, two major factors should be considered. First, with cases of multiple murder, dismemberment, or any particularly grotesque act that represents the bizarre or horrible, results are more positive for the defendant when tried before a judge. These types of highly deviant acts illicit much stronger emotional reactions from lay people than from judges. Furthermore, the judge has greater accountability for his or her legal rulings than do jurors.

Second, you may consider avoiding a jury trial in the case of a notorious, very unpleasant, or extremely unattractive defendant. If juries visually find the defendant attractive, they are more lenient than if they view the defendant as unattractive.

Judges typically decide the case after assessing the facts, and the ancillary social issues should have very little effect on the outcome. Juries, on the other hand, place a great deal of weight on the social issues. Your decision should be based on the strengths and weaknesses of your case.

FIRST MEETING WITH CLIENT

Trial preparation for you, the client, and the witnesses begins with the first meeting. During the first meeting you and your client are forming impressions of each other that may last throughout your relationship When the first meeting is in your office, the setting gives you formal control over the situation. The client is on your ground (territorial space), allowing you to focus on the merits of the case.

Illustration (3.1a) shows a formal setting in the attorney's office (notice the desk as a blocking device). The psychological principle of desk territory is that the owner controls the two-thirds of his desk nearest him, and the visitor has access to the other one-third. The power of territorial space, timing, professional image, and credentialed authority resides with the attorney in this setting.

FIRST MEETING

3.1a
• Formal Setting
• Social to Public Zone

SECOND MEETING WITH CLIENT

I recommend that your second meeting be one of leisure, informality, meaning, and depth. The client should do most of the speaking. Be sure that your leisure seating arrangement provides a total view of the client from shoes to hairstyle [Illustration (3.1b)]. You will be completing a mental picture of the client as a courtroom participant and gaining an understanding of how others will view the client during testimony. You are:

1. Assessing the visual impact of your client on others. Does he or she present an image compatible with the outcome or settlement size desired?
2. Determining whether the client is telling the truth.
3. Assessing whether the client comes across to others as a truthful or honest person.
4. Letting the client speak freely in order to be more comfortable. Open-ended questions and free associations often yield information that may be otherwise unattainable.
5. Assessing the client's communication style for strengths and weaknesses to be integrated into trial strategy for maximum effect.

Many of the complaints that are leveled against attorneys have to do with the attorney's personality and how the attorney handles the client. Clients are like jurors: if they do not like someone they do not mind punishing him.

3.1b
• Relaxed Setting
• Personal to Social Zones
• No Blocking Devices

INTERVIEWING

You acquire language, values, attitudes, and numerous functional skills while receiving your formal education. During the first six months of your professional working career, you acquire a large percentage of your day-to-day habits. As you develop the necessary skills of an effective trial lawyer, you also learn numerous "bad" habits, which may be continued throughout your career. Interviewing is an integral part of your legal practice; when expertly done it provides you with invaluable information and insight. Yet few practicing attorneys enter their careers in possession of interviewing expertise.

Interviewing should never be a mechanical process of simply obtaining facts or information. Essential variables in the interviewing process are as often visual as they are verbal. A few of the visual and verbal relationship enhancers, which can be used in the interview situation, will be reviewed for those lawyers with a limited interviewing background. (In this regard, the enhancement techniques offered by Arnold Goldstein in *Helping People Change* can be very useful.) Essentially, when your client has a close identification with you, he is more open, is more likely to explore ideas and alternatives, and is more likely to follow your advice.

Psychological structuring includes numerous techniques that can be used by the attorney to increase client, witness, or juror rapport. Telling a client that he will have a positive and educational experience on the witness stand is an example of direct structuring. The client is being oriented to look for the positive aspects of a particular situation. Psychologically, the greater your positive attitude toward an experience the less impact negative events will have.

Role structuring involves realistically clarifying for the client exactly what will happen in the courtroom or in the witness box. When the mystery is removed from future events, the person will be more relaxed and alert and will exhibit quicker and more complete recall. In other words, structuring furthers a relaxed demeanor, improves cognitive functioning, and creates a positive feeling toward the person doing the structuring. Courtesy instructions to the jury during the opening statements have this effect.

Clients and witnesses will have a greater tendency to see you as highly credible if you project a totally professional image. Diplomas and honors are hung on office walls in order to enhance your image as a professional. A large part of the professional image is observable in dress and body language. Behavioral indicators that increase professional credibility are:

1. Shaking the client's hand with your hips directly parallel to the other person and greeting him by his first name. The habit of greeting someone across your desk or shaking hands with your body angled at 45 degrees or 90 degrees tells the other person in "body language" that he isn't important enough to receive a complete greeting.

2. A neat but not stuffy appearance.
3. Addressing the other person at his eye level. In most cases eye level is effectively enhanced by sitting down.
4. Maintaining an attentive demeanor and letting the client finish speaking without interruptions.
5. Using warm, relaxed facial expressions and open hand gestures.
6. Using fluent, confident speech, which comes from being prepared.
7. Asking direct, focused questions that follow a logical progression.
8. Permitting the client to do most of the talking during informational interviews.
9. Avoiding "lower class" posture or slouching.
10. Using a warm voice tone; avoidance of flat, effortless, monotonous voices.
11. Providing a relaxed, comfortable environment.

Combining visual and verbal elements in client interviews can significantly increase the quality of information. Visual communication, demeanor, and body language all represent important parts of effective interviewing. Blatantly misusing any of the above eleven suggestions may decrease meaningful communication, increase the psychological distance between parties, and lower your credibility.

TEAM IMAGE

In both civil and criminal cases, you should plan to make the verbal and visual communication consistent throughout the trial. In terms of dress, for example, you would not want your client dressed in a three-piece suit one day, a blazer the next, and a sweater on the third. One step up or down on the dress continuum is the maximum acceptable range. Wide variations along the dress continuum elicit an inordinate amount of attention, act as detractors, and tend to sidetrack the main focus of the jurors. Conversely, dress and image detractors can be used to deemphasize verbal and cognitive materials.

John C. Shepherd, past president of the ABA, holds numerous awards and honors as a trial lawyer. Mr. Shepherd shows his awareness of the impact of image by using a wooden pencil instead of a gold pen in front of some juries. (You might note that Johnny Carson uses the same types of techniques.) Image, acceptance, and identification are critical in the development and maintenance of credibility with the jury.

When preparing your client, be specific. Asking your client to "look good," to "dress up," or even to "wear a tie" is not adequate. Ties could be slip ties, suits could be loud or inappropriate, women may wear a pant suit rather than a skirted one, and the list goes on and on. The client needs to know precisely what to wear and the reasoning behind the instruction. It is important for clients to understand how their image fits into the overall trial strategy. Your clients should be aware of the following general points:

1. A good visual image should be shown to the jury throughout the trial. The first few minutes of visual contact, however, are the most critical in that first impressions are both long lasting and elicit emotions that influence future attitudes and perceptions about that individual.
2. In criminal cases, the defendant's overall appearance should be inconsistent with the crime. The objective is to have the jury look at the client and make a visual assessment that makes a relationship between crime and criminal seem incompatible.
3. In civil cases your client should look like he or she could use the amount of money under consideration and that he or she deserves it. Affluent-looking people get smaller settlements from middle-class juries.
4. A conservative social and professional image is generally recommended. Clothes should be neutral, hair styles moderate, jewelry toned down, footwear compatible with clothing, and overall appearance consistent throughout the trial.

Facial hair may have a negative effect, and the more radical the beard, mustache, or sideburns, the greater the undesirable effect.

WITNESS ORIENTATION

When you meet with witnesses, ask them to go over everything they know about the case and let them talk freely. If witnesses leave after only answering your specific questions, you may wind up being surprised during the trial. Consequently, open-ended questions should be used liberally.

Witnesses should know what questions you will be asking them. You want no confusion and no surprises when your witnesses are testifying. When a trial has been delayed for weeks or months, it is important to meet personally with witnesses again to review dress, image, expectations, and procedures. It is also a good idea to have three phone numbers for witnesses—home, work, and a friend. It is wise for witnesses to be in the courtroom an hour or two before they testify. This relieves some of the tension of the alien environment (territorial space identification) and creates a higher level of psychological comfort. After sitting in the courtroom for an hour or more, they will have adjusted to the territory and be will able to concentrate on the interaction between participants.

It is easy for seasoned courtroom practitioners to forget how stressful a court appearance can be to lay people. If witnesses experience a great deal of stress, their image will be "tarnished" as a result of disorganized answers and erratic responses. Witnesses are apprehensive about what will happen to them during cross-examination. Attorneys who fail to prepare witnesses for cross-examination risk the possibility of those witnesses losing credibility with the jury. I suggest that the following points be covered as part of the total witness preparation:

1. Instruct witnesses to tell the truth regardless of who is asking the question and to answer questions to the best of their ability. Inform them that you will be able to address, at a later time, any negative aspects that may be brought out through cross-examination. Once the witnesses recognize that they do not have to outthink the cross-examiner, they will become much more relaxed about testifying.

Well-prepared witnesses have a greater total understanding of the situation, which increases their confidence and credibility.

One of the most detrimental things witnesses can do is to attempt to shade the facts for one side. The more truthfully witnesses explain the facts, the greater their credibility with the jury.

2. Witnesses should be instructed not to over-answer questions. This tendency is the greatest when they have given statements they feel are damaging to the client's case. Witnesses usually get caught in the adversary's trap when they begin going beyond basic answers. Well-prepared witnesses will not assist the opposition by needlessly elaborating or by dodging specific questions.

WITNESS DRESS

Witnesses' dress should complement their courtroom roles, as well as being compatible with the overall trial strategy. You cannot be too careful or specific about witness dress instructions. Witnesses frequently have only one exposure to the jury and it is paramount that it be the correct one. I recommend that counsel:

1. Explain to witnesses specifically what they should wear. Discuss their overall appearance with them and find out exactly what items are available in their wardrobe.
2. Explain trial strategy and how their desired appearance fits into that strategy.
3. Explain that witnesses should avoid clothing, jewelry, hair styles, or makeup that will call their credibility into question or become distracting during examination, especially radical, modish, or sexually oriented items.
4. Explain that witness speech style and general vocabulary should be natural and unaffected. This is not the time to try out a new vocabulary or "accent." You can relieve considerable anxiety for most witnesses by telling them to just be themselves on the witness stand.

Witnesses, like clients, are frequently reluctant to change hair styles, makeup, or clothing, which is why you must fully explain their part in the total trial strategy.

EXPERTS AND UNIFORMS

Expert witnesses should normally wear a form of power dress at or near the top of the "power dress continuum." For males this could entail wearing a dark gray or blue three-piece suit, white shirt, plain executive shoes, and a foulard or club tie. A similar conservative skirted suit is recommended for women with a plain white blouse, heels, and conservative makeup. If the woman has long hair it should be worn up in a businesslike style. Expert witness dress should be adjusted on the continuum to be compatible with different geographical parts of the country and to accommodate differences in rural-urban tastes.

Nonexpert witnesses can comfortably dress at the upper limit of their social class. A blue collar worker who wears an executive three-piece suit will draw attention to himself rather than to his testimony. The ideal is to have each person look like a neat, conservative version of his or her social or occupational group.

WITNESS UNIFORM

3.2a
• Increased Authoritative Image
• Only Police Can Wear This Uniform

3.2b
• Decreased Authoritative Image
• Anybody Can Wear a Suit

Research supports the position that uniforms increase the credibility of most witnesses (3.2a) and (3.2b). Recent studies indicate that police testimony is one of the biggest factors in criminal trials. Juries believe police officers, so have them in uniform if possible. If a police officer made the arrest in uniform it would be best for her to wear that uniform while giving testimony. Psychologically it is easier for jurors to place the officer back at the scene of the crime. If the officer completed an investigation as a plainclothes detective it would be unnatural to have her testify in a patrol officer's uniform.

Similar recommendations are in order for other uniformed people in a variety of medical and other service occupations. A nurse appears more credible in her uniform than she does in a dress. The same holds true for postal carriers, ambulance drivers, security guards, and other uniformed professionals.

TRIAL PREPARATION OUTLINE

The trial preparation outline was developed for two reasons: (1) to help you organize your case and to increase your overall trial effectiveness; and (2) to be a guide to show you if you are ready to present your case to a jury. If, as you work through the outline, there are areas you cannot answer or areas you are not completely sure of, flag those trouble areas and solve them before the trial. It is a good practice to go through this outline as soon as you have all your evidence complete and then again a few weeks before trial and finally, as a final review, a week before the trial.

Chart IV

TRIAL PREPARATION OUTLINE

FIRM _____

ATTORNEY _____

CASE FILE NUMBER _____

CAUSE OF ACTION _____

PLAINTIFF (　)　　　　　　　DEFENDANT (　)

    I. CLIENTS (YOUR CLIENT—THEIR CLIENT)
        A. BACKGROUND
            1. Name
            2. Address
            3. Occupation
            4. Gender
            5. National Origin
            6. Age
            7. Marital Status
            8. Reputation in Community
        B. STRENGTHS
            1.
            2.
        C. WEAKNESSES
            1.
            2.

II. LEGAL ELEMENTS OF CASE
    A.
    B.
    C.
III. CASE: LEGAL AND SOCIAL
    A. STRENGTHS OF YOUR CASE
        1.
        2.
        3.
        4.
    B. WEAKNESSES OF YOUR CASE
        1.
        2.
        3.
    C. STRENGTHS OF THEIR CASE
        1.
        2.
        3.
        4.
    D. WEAKNESSES OF THEIR CASE
        1.
        2.
        3.
IV. JURY INSTRUCTIONS
    A. SPECIFIC INSTRUCTIONS
        1.
        2.
    B. SPECIAL INTERROGATORIES TO JURY
        1.
        2.
        3.

V. VERDICT SOUGHT
    A. CRIMINAL CASE
        1. Acquittal
        2. Hung Jury
        3. Lesser Included Offense
        4. Conviction
    B. CIVIL CASE
        1. Remedies Sought
            (a) Compensatory, High or Low
            (b) Punitive, High or Low

VI. THREE MAIN POINTS OF OPENING AND CLOSING STATEMENTS
    A.
    B.
    C.

VII. PROFILE OF IDEAL JUROR
    A. PSYCHOLOGICAL:
        1. Emotional-Technical
        2. Structured-Unstructured
        3. Leader-Follower
    B. GENDER:
        1. Male-Female
    C. AGE:
        1. Young-Middle-Old
    D. RACE
    E. OCCUPATION:
        1. Individual-Group
        2. Things-People
    F. ECONOMIC:
        1. Upper-Middle-Lower
    G. EDUCATION:
        1. High-Low
        2. Formal-Trade

H. DRESS:
   1. Formal-Informal
   2. Style
   3. Congruent-Incongruent with Status
I. BODY LANGUAGE:
   1. Aggressive-Passive
   2. Open-Closed
J. HOBBIES:
   1. Active-Passive
   2. Individual-Group
K. ORGANIZATIONS:
   1. Professional-Social-Athletic
   2. Officer-Member Only
   3. No Involvement
L. MARITAL STATUS:
   1. Single-Married-Widowed-Divorced
M. CHILDREN:
   1. Young-Old
   2. Number
   3. None
N. RESIDENCE:
   1. Owner-House or Condo
   2. Renter-House or Apartment
O. OTHER: If applicable
   1. Religion, Alcohol, Drugs, Handicapped
VIII. JUROR PROFILE TO STRIKE
   A.
   B.
   C.
   D.
   E.

IX. VOIR DIRE QUESTIONS
    A. Obtaining Information on Jurors
        1. Personality
        2. Family
        3. Employment
        4. History
        5. Other (as needed)
    B. Planting Seeds of Case
        1. Using Buzz Words
        2. Planting Doubt
        3. Case Theory
    C. Gaining Rapport
        1. Fair to Both Sides
        2. Decide Case Only on Merits
        3. If They Want to Serve
X. EVIDENCE
    A. YOUR WITNESS
        1. Expert
        2. Character
        3. Lay
    B. METHOD OF PRESENTATION
        1. Oral
        2. Documentary
        3. Charts/Graphs
        4. Audio/Video
        5. Photographic
    C. APPEARANCE
        1. Dress
        2. Demeanor
    D. SUPPORT OPENING/CLOSING STATEMENT

XI. THEIR WITNESSES
  A. WHAT THEIR TESTIMONY WILL SHOW
  B. HOW THEIR TESTIMONY WILL BE PRESENTED
    1. Oral
    2. Documentary
    3. Other
  C. COUNTERING OR USING THEIR TESTIMONY
    1. Destroy
    2. Neutralize
    3. Impeach
    4. Reinforcing (if it aids your case)
  D. AREAS TO AVOID
    1. Nondamaging areas
  E. ENDING CROSS-EXAMINATION
    1. Witnesses' Major Weakness

SUMMARY

A great confidence builder for you and your witnesses is the knowledge that your team is thoroughly prepared for the trial. Confidence builds credibility by relaxing trial participants and permitting them to focus on the procedures at hand, not on their tension or misgivings. Furthermore, a thoroughly prepared and relaxed team is better prepared to handle unforseen problems.

Chapter 4 will cover voir dire—from related jury statistics to the assessment of jurors by the use of the Rasicot Personality Classification System.

VOIR DIRE

HISTORY

The "radical" concept that the common man could participate in the state's legal system originated with the Athenian Solon (638-599 B.C.). Roman conquerors brought these ideas to the Anglo-Saxons, and by the eleventh and twelfth centuries William the Conqueror and Henry II had undertaken their codification of English law. "Inquests" or "inquisitions" became the early precursors of colonial America's jury system. In English law, the question of how to achieve community participation was established by the Magna Carta; peers of the defendant were required as jurors.

By American standards, the English communities were populated by people with well-established traditions and very little geographical mobility. The class structure was rigid, and social change was not even a meaningful concept. The colonization of North America changed these parameters and produced numerous new forces to modify America's legal inheritance. For example, the American frontier took hundreds of years to close and covered distances uncommon to the English. Consequently, the attorney's role became more prominent because someone familiar with problems of procedure, jury idiosyncracies, and court personnel was needed.

In 1774 the first Continental Congress established the right to trial by "peers of defendant." Differences between the practices established by each of the thirteen colonies are still evident in our contemporary system. We have, over the years, however, established some basic guidelines:

1. Juries should be composed of impartial citizens picked at random.
2. No particular jurors are specified, but competent, fair, and impartial jurors are required.
3. The jury selection process should produce conscientious, fair-minded jurors and eliminate those with prejudice and other undesirable characteristics.

THREE PURPOSES OF VOIR DIRE

1. The overt purpose of voir dire is to attain an "unbiased" jury. Given the human condition that feelings and attitudes retain supremacy over reason, the best you can expect is relative impartiality. Nevertheless, prospective jurors must clearly understand the idea of impartiality and the goal of rendering a verdict according to the facts rather than individualized feelings and biases. In the practical situation, your job is to eliminate those jurors who would be most damaging to your case. With practice, you can learn to use visual and verbal indicators in eliminating those who will be most detrimental to your case.

There are two covert purposes of voir dire:

2. Establishing rapport between jury members and your team, and
3. Planting the seeds of your case.

JUDGE OR LAWYER QUESTIONING

If the judge asks the voir dire questions, the prospect is that the total selection time will be drastically shortened. It can also be argued that counsel will not be able to plant the seeds of their case if questioning is left to the judiciary. In 1990 California passed Proposition 115, which changed the state courts to judge-conducted questioning during voir dire. During voir dire state judges in California, like all federal judges, may or may not allow the attorneys to question jurors.

On counsel's behalf it is argued that voir dire is the only time they have for direct interaction with the jurors and they deserve this opportunity. Furthermore, it is likely that trial attorneys will have a more intimate knowledge of the case than the judge; therefore, the attorneys are the best persons to question jurors about specific biases that may damage their case.

The Rasicot visual system of jury selection can be used whether a judge or a lawyer does the questioning and can even be used if no questions are asked of the panel. Recently we completely waived asking questions in a trial, surprising our adversaries. This was done for a number of reasons relating to the specific case:

1. We already knew from visual factors and background whom we wanted to excuse.
2. Our adversary was not yet sure whom to strike. (His questioning was finished).
3. We did not want opposing counsel to have any more information about jurors as a result of our questioning.
4. We wanted to appear as "Mr. Niceguy" in contrast to our opponent's aggressive style. In this case the bonuses of not asking questions outweighed the negatives. The plan was successful enough that our adversary actually struck a person we had planned to excuse. The case was settled before it went to the jury.

JURY SELECTION PRELIMINARIES

Ideal questions during jury selection should accomplish three purposes:

1. Obtain background information about jurors
2. Gain rapport with jurors
3. Indirectly plant the seeds of your case

It is important to know exactly what you are looking for before you ask a question. The answers should help you decide if the person is either an ideal or an unwanted juror.

Another goal that you can strive for during voir dire is to convince the jurors to verbally and mentally commit themselves to a way of thinking or to a particular verdict if the facts support it. (Empirical evidence supports the impression that jurors tend to organize subsequent trial facts according to their initial impressions.)

Voir dire is an excellent opportunity to initiate your visual assessment of the jurors and place them into preliminary personality groups. You can also gain insights into how you can best develop positive relationships with jurors and ascertain who the likely jury foreperson will be.

Open-ended questions are useful during voir dire because they increase the amount of visual as well as verbal communication you receive. For example, words that reference the person speaking, such as "I" versus "we," indicate dominance or assertiveness. The extensive use of gestures tells you that the person tends to control his or her personal space. First-person answers demonstrate a sense of personal responsibility, whereas third-person responses indicate an inclination to accept group decisions.

As you practice "reading" the patterns of jurors' and witnesses' body language, it becomes increasingly easier to detect dominant, neutral, or submissive signals, which help assess the jurors' personality grouping. Verbal questioning of the panel will provide counsel with normal insights in addition to personality information. If you visually assess a person to be technical and critical, and he informs you verbally that he is an engineer or accountant, you confirm your assumptions. If he has technical hobbies such as ship building or reading very technical books, you have additional confirmation of your initial assessment.

If you approaches voir dire as a strictly technical procedure, opportunities to enhance rapport will slip by.

TEN "DO'S" OF VOIR DIRE

1. Advise jurors on prying questions. Tell the jury in the beginning you are not there to pry into their personal lives out of curiosity, but that it is your duty to find a fair and impartial jury to decide this important case.
2. Explain trial procedures. People are usually stressful when involved in a situation with which they are unfamiliar and do not know what is about to happen. Some of this tension can be relieved if the

jury understands the different parts of the trial and how it fits together. If you are the one to help them relieve this tension, through a brief explanation, you will enhance your positive rapport with them. Comprehension increases when tension decreases and vice versa.

3. Prepare your questions. Ask as many open-ended questions as you need, but know what answers you are looking for. Every question should have a purpose. Open-ended questions give you more time to visually and verbally assess the entire response.

4. Make it interesting. Skip around the panel and keep the process moving. It is more work for you to organize the questioning, but with practice it will become a smooth presentation.

5. Use simple questions and simple language. Any time jurors have to admit they did not understand you it is embarrassing to them. If your questions are multifaceted or overly technical, they won't expand upon an idea they do not understand.

6. Show fairness and compliment the jurors. Fairness is one of the biggest factors in establishing credibility. As part of the process of developing rapport with jurors, it is helpful to give a compliment if it is natural and in context. For example, in response to the question "Do you belong to any groups?" a prospective juror answers, "Yes, A.A., I've been dry for seven years!" This person is obviously proud of his accomplishment and a short compliment is in order. If you keep an open mind at such times, future rapport can be greatly enhanced.

7. Use jurors' names and be polite. Always use jurors' names when addressing them and use "please" and "thank you" when appropriate. Courtesy, like fairness, is reciprocal and strengthens rapport.

8. Maintain eye contact. When jurors are speaking, show them they have your complete attention. People will talk one-third longer if you have good eye contact and nod your head up and down as in agreement. The longer they talk the more information they give out.

9. Present a sincere, credible image. You may have conducted dozens, if not hundreds of voir dires, but the jury has only this one to relate to. It is comparable to a doctor who delivers a baby to first-

time parents—he has gone through this weekly but he should show some excitement and caring to the proud parents. It is important to project a genuine concern for justice throughout the case.
10. Have voir dire recorded. Protect the record in case any number of legal questions arise out of challenges or actual questioning.

TEN "DON'TS" OF VOIR DIRE

1. Don't prove your brilliance. Ninety percent of the jurors think you're smarter than they are anyway. Overtly showing mental superiority is "overkill" and produces negative rapport. Conversely, communicating on their level enhances rapport and strengthens credibility.
2. Don't use "legalese." Understanding your presentation is the key to the trial; the less the jurors understand, the less effective your case.
3. Don't embarrass the jurors. This usually occurs in areas of education (Why didn't you finish your degree?), occupation (I see you have worked for XYZ Company for six years and haven't moved from your entry position; don't you get along with the management?), marriage (You have indicated you have three teenage children and you are single, how long have you been divorced?). Granted, you would like to know the answers to some of these questions and they may be of assistance to you, but the negative impact may be too explosive. In some directly related cases this information may be essential; the overall picture must be evaluated.
4. Don't tell "war stories." Keep the jurors concentrating on your case and not on your past achievements, unless the theme of the story is directly focused on a main idea of your case.
5. Don't use humor. Humor sets a light mood and by nature it is poking fun at someone or something. It is important to show a sense of humor when something spontaneously happens, but do not work it into your case. One lawyer I work with likes to have everyone in the jury laugh at least once during voir dire; he feels it relaxes them and strengthens his rapport. He has a very special personality and is

gifted enough to get positive reactions most of the time. Keep in mind, however, that no one is turned off because you don't add humor, but someone may be turned off if they feel offended or resentful.

6. Don't concentrate on any one juror. Don't use one juror to plant all your seeds and another to gain rapport with the jury. Even though they all hear the answers, people like to be spoken to, they like to be spoken about, they like to look at themselves, and they like to talk. You won't find them all equally pleasing or interesting, but you want each one to get the feeling he is a very important person. In the end you will treat them all as very important persons, so be consistent.

7. Don't take notes while questioning. Make prospective jurors feel they are having a relaxed conversation with you rather than a police interrogation. The less eye contact you have with them, the fewer visual signals you can interpret. A jury selection consultant stated that he had five pages of body language notes on one juror during a ten minute questioning. How many signals did he miss while he was writing? If you know your material and know what you are looking for, writing a few "buzz" words after questioning will bring back the overall impression.

8. Don't argue with the jurors. Inquire into their positions without placing values on their answers. If there is an argument, three things may happen:
   (a) They will change their position to keep from being further embarrassed and "get even" with you later
   (b) The rest of their answers will be severely shortened to eliminate any further conflicts
   (c) They may strengthen their point of view and poison other members of the jury
   In all three cases, you are the loser even if that person is removed.

9. Don't gamble on a one-person jury. A very strong person may change his mind halfway through the trial as a result of an unexpected event. It's a real gamble, and only in very rare cases is it worth the chance.

10. Don't take the first twelve jurors. This is usually as bad as the one-person jury. Even if everyone is appropriate for your case, you want a chance to eliminate those people who won't synergistically fit the rest of the group.

CHALLENGES

There are two major types of challenges: to the array and to individuals. Challenges to the entire panel come first, and parties who initiate the challenge to the array have the burden of offering supporting evidence. Challenges to the array tend to be of a technical nature and generally represent deviations from statutory procedures.

Challenges to individual jurors are of two types: challenge for cause and peremptory challenge. Some of the general challenges for cause are:

1. The juror is related to a party of the litigation
2. The juror has a unique interest in the subject matter
3. The juror has served in a related case or on a grand jury that indicted the accused
4. The juror has a state of mind that will prevent him or her from acting with impartiality and without prejudice to the substantial rights of either party (Jordan 1980, 54-55)

The number of challenges for cause is unlimited and in many ways is bound only by the creative imagination of the examiner. Peremptory challenges need not be defended once established by the state legislature, as long as statutory provisions have been followed. "Once a peremptory challenge is granted by the legislature, however, the right to that challenge is definite and absolute, and cannot be denied." My focus in this section is on peremptory challenges and on whom to use them.

JURY FOREPERSON

Jury forepersons will direct and be responsible for about 25 percent of the total participation during deliberation. The typical jury foreperson is a male in 70 percent of the cases. He is very talkative, personable, confident, and above average in intelligence (*Trial Diplomacy Journal,* Spring 1982).

During jury selection you need to determine two types of dominant individuals who are potential jury forepersons. Forepersons usually fall into the "green" or "red" classifications. In those instances where the jury foreperson is chosen by lot and is not a red or green personality, the chosen foreperson acts primarily as a figurehead. (Interviews with jurors after trials have been completed confirm this position from my trial experiences.)

Look at the jury and ask yourself "If we had an emergency situation, which juror would we rely on to solve the problem for all of us?" If you are a good judge of character, you probably will be right in picking the foreperson 75 percent of the time. Remember, jurors select a foreperson whom they respect.

JURY STATISTICS

Juries are expensive in that they cost the nation about two hundred million dollars in fees annually and another billion dollars in lost wages. Approximately one-third of the three million jurors who are called nationally each year never sit on a case (*Time,* Sept. 28, 1981). Furthermore, in states like New York, about one-third of the time spent on criminal cases is for jury selection.

Jury instruction research supported the position that it was best for the defense when the judge reminded the jury before the trial began that accused criminals are innocent until proven guilty. When this occurred, 37 percent of one hundred subject jurors found the defendant guilty, as compared to 59 percent when the reminder was received at the end of the trial and 63 percent with no reminder at all. Those who received reminders prior to the trial also paid more attention during the trial and remembered the facts better (*Psychology Today,* June 1980, 30). Judges telling the jury about the presumption of evidence have a much greater effect than lawyers providing the same information. The credibility of the judiciary is much greater than that of the attorney. Jurors respect judges and believe they are neutral and have nothing to gain or lose in the case. Therefore jurors believe the judge when she tells them something.

Once jury members have formulated their initial impressions of the case, they tend to agree with those facts that are consistent with their initial impression and disagree or dismiss facts that are incompatible with this initial viewpoint as being unreliable, erroneous, or unrepresentative (Herbert, 1982, 207). Emotions clearly color which facts will be given the most weight in the juror's final decision. In that initial impressions are formulated in the first few minutes of contact, the importance of image becomes apparent. The visual and nonverbal variables operating during the trial take on new meanings when you review the social and behavioral science data.

As the following study indicates, jury selection only partially reduces decision bias. The following information is taken from a study of sixty-five jurors from ten trials:

1. Seventy-eight percent of the jurors were unsure of guilt or innocence at the beginning of the trials; 22 percent had already made up their minds before the trials began.
2. Fifty-nine percent of the jurors based their decisions on trial facts; 41 percent based their "conscious" decisions on something else.
3. Twenty-three percent made their final decision during deliberations.
4. Police testimony was generally the most important factor determining guilt or innocence (*Human Behavior,* April, 1979). Testimony by uniformed police officers is often a major persuasion factor in both civil and criminal cases.

INTRODUCTION TO VISUAL PERSONALITY ASSESSMENT

The Rasicot system of personality assessment uses background information, verbal responses, and a preponderance of visual indicators that are observable and generally free from the bias of polite verbal answers. For example, if I ask if you are comfortable around people who are physically deformed or handicapped, the polite answer is "yes." You have responded according to social expectation, though you may indeed be biased and uncomfortable in the presence of those who are physically different. In a similar fashion, attempting to predict juror bias or prejudice through verbal examination is equally fraught with limitations, as well as being terribly time consuming.

Compare the verbal assessment process with the visual system. If you ask the same question about another's feelings toward handicapped people and his answer is delayed, his demeanor changes, and physically he shows tension, will you now accept the verbal or the visual response as being most accurate? When you receive many double messages (verbal answers that differ from visual responses), there is a natural tendency to be somewhat confused in the interpretation of the real meanings. In these cases you usually follow your intuition or "gut level" feelings but can't really explain why you feel this way.

The Rasicot system assists you in understanding your "gut feelings" by explaining each factor and how it fits into the overall impression. The polygraph was developed in order to circumvent the limitations of verbal communication and substitute objective behavioral indicators. The Rasicot method of personality assessment is similar to a visual polygraph.

The intent of voir dire examination is to find impartial, fair-minded people. You want to know their reactions to specific people, things, or events. Being able to read body language or demeanor, in addition to your ability to analyze verbal answers, significantly increases your powers of assessment. In addition to expanding your powers of assessment regarding individual questions, the Rasicot method will provide considerable insight into the basic personality orientation of others. When you gain expertise in these visual tools you will be able to assess others along the dimensions of: active or passive, followers or leaders, technical or emotional, generous or conservative, and many other factors of importance to you.

Remember, I am not claiming to have produced a perfect system. I do know from practice and research, though, that the visual techniques discussed herein greatly enhance total communication and overall accuracy.

Nonverbal communicators such as dress, demeanor, and space usage usually reflect a subconscious personality. These indicators are generally more indicative of people's internal psychological state than are their socially modified verbal answers. The important thing to remember is that you want to understand all of the personality clues that each juror is giving you. Even when voir dire is severely restricted, you can still visually assess jurors in addition to gleaning basic information from the juror questionnaire. The more clues you are able to use the more accurate you will be.

PERSONALITIES AND COLOR

I have included this section on color psychology for three reasons: (1) color psychology theories have been around for the last fifty years, but within the last ten years there have been major breakthroughs showing how colors affect people; (2) there is a very high correlation between certain colors and certain personality types; and (3) it is an technique I have found very useful in the courtroom to classify a large group of people very quickly. Their general color preferences are only one small clue added to the many other clues to place them in a certain color category.

COLOR PSYCHOLOGY

Max Lüscher is the famous Swiss psychologist whose color tests and studies are widely used around the world. Lüscher's color psychology is applied to areas as diverse as vocational guidance and personnel selection as well as medical and psychological diagnosis. The review of his works and related studies is time consuming and technical, but for those with a background in psychology and the social sciences it is highly interesting. In this section you will be given an overview extensive enough so that, combined with my research and experiential modifications, everyday application will be possible.

Lüscher found that each color has the same physiological effect on people from all over the world. The colors of nature are a deep-seated part of your primitive personality. The autonomic nervous system controls your digestive processes, heartbeat, glandular functions, and other basic body maintenance activities. Colors have a direct effect on the autonomic nervous system. In a macro-patterned sense, you have been shaped by your environment during the course of human evolution. Dark colors (blue and green) slow down your heartbeat and breathing and lower your blood pressure.

The opposite of the colors of the night are the colors of day red and yellow. The lighter colors have the opposite effect on your autonomic nervous system. They increase your heartbeat, turn up your metabolic rate, and generally make you ready for "the day's activities."

The light and dark of your daily cycle is part of the universal human condition. All normal infants first learn to distinguish bright and dark contrasts, then movement, and finally shape and form. Physical reactions to colors hold true whether or not you are color blind; hence color response tests hold true even for those who have handicapped color vision. The colors' individual hues are still interpreted by the brain even though you may be visually color blind.

The four primary colors are a basic and primitive part of the brain's evolutionary development. Colors are also part of your active learning: a part of the educated brain we call the central nervous system. We all develop color preferences.

STRUCTURE AND FUNCTION OF COLOR

Functional psychology is the name given to those theories correlating color choice with personality types. The "structure" of a color is constant and is defined as the "objective" meaning of that color. The objective meaning of a color remains the same for everyone. Dark blue, for instance, elicits relaxation and tranquility, regardless of whether you like or dislike that color; red and yellow elicit activity and stimulate the autonomic nervous system.

The "function" of color is the subjective attitude toward the color, and this functional attitude can vary from person to person. The structure of the color physical reaction is the same for all people. Lighter colors increase internal activity and darker colors decrease internal activity. The function of a color psychological reaction is whether you like or dislike the feeling that the color gives you. It is like music, in that acid rock music is activity-producing and mellow music is relaxing. Different people prefer different styles of music because they enjoy the mood it helps to create. Most of us enjoy several different kinds of music at different times, but we still have our overall favorite style. This is the same situation with colors. You may change your short-term color preference, but overall you have a main color orientation that parallels your basic personality.

Red, yellow, blue, and green are "psychological primaries" and constitute the four basic color groupings. Violet, brown, gray, and black are "auxiliary colors." Violet, brown, gray, and black are "color blends" and can be used for a more in-depth personality analysis.

The effect of a specific color on the autonomic nervous system is similar for all people. Consequently, if you are emotionally or physically in need of peace and quiet and release from tension and stress, the darker colors will help fulfill this need and are therefore preferred. Conversely, if you desire to dissipate energy either physically or mentally, the innate response is to choose brighter colors. Environmental circumstances can temporarily alter your color preferences, and color preferences, like any other learned behavior, can and do change over time. You need to remember two important points:

1. Color preference patterns are more important than the choice of any one specific color. Notice jury patterns throughout the trial. Who is wearing the bright colors and who is wearing the darker colors? Who is wearing the wild or ornate clothing and who is wearing the conservative clothing? As with other aspects of visual com-

munication, I have asked you to observe patterns more carefully than any one specific visual or nonverbal characteristic.

2. Prediction of a person's behavior is more accurate when you can identify his specific moods. Psychologists who try to predict future behavior by using a one-time assessment are constantly thwarted because of situational or environmental mood changes. Being able to evaluate the jury throughout the trial will give you a more accurate final assessment than doing an initial assessment during voir dire and assuming it will remain the same. Consequently, it is germane to the central thesis of this argument that visual indicators are more apropos to assessing a person's changing personality states than are the verbal answers given during voir dire. In the courtroom you want to understand the jurors' behavior changes, if any, and to predict their behavior pattern at the end of the trial. During a talk show from Washington, D.C., concerning the Hinkley verdict I stated that had the lawyers assessed behavioral patterns throughout the trial, the verdict should not have come as a surprise. The situation was similar in the *Texaco* case: lawyers were involved with a jury for months and were not be able to recognize their pent-up anger.

Color psychology is used in medicine, counseling, personnel work, psychological diagnosis, and geriatrics as well as in numerous other areas in addition to the Rasicot system of jury selection.

LÜSCHER'S PRIMARY COLOR PERSONALITY TYPES

In order to focus on the specific application of color psychology to personality types, I will discuss general characteristics of people who prefer the primary colors of red, yellow, blue, and green. We all are a blend of all four of these colors, but one is usually more dominant than the other three. The higher the color dominance, the more characteristic traits will be exhibited. Each color has strong and weak points, so there is no good or bad group, simply different orientations.

Practice placing people in certain groups and see how your accuracy improves. Start with your family and friends and use the charts to assess the different facets of their personalities.

Red

The color red elicits activity and excitement, and those who prefer red are expressing competitiveness and independence. Personality types that we call "reds" are active doers. A list of their general characteristics, along with characteristics associated with other primary color personality types, follows in Charts V and VI. The red personality, whether male or female, is independent, competitive, a leader, and seeks continuous challenge.

Reds expand the space around them with aggressive gestures and body movements. Their voice modulations are loud and harsh, and they quickly assert dominance over territorial space. They are less concerned about dress, hair styles, and jewelry than the other groups. Their speech is very short and direct; they are poor listeners and are very impatient. They pay little attention to detail and prefer the overall picture. They are decision makers. Reds are task oriented and will concentrate on one task until it is accomplished and then start another. Reds are generally very independent and have strong personalities. These are the people both sides in a case recognize a potential one-person juries. Red corresponds to the fire in life.

Yellow

Yellow is the lightest and the most active color. Yellows like to intellectually impress others. Individuals who prefer yellow are adventurous but unlike reds, very gregarious. They are expansive, prefer free and liberating experiences, and tend to be uninhibited. They are very free thinking and optimistic, but start more projects than they can finish.

Yellows (Chart V) are visibly fashion oriented, bubbly, romantic, optimistic, and sociable. They speak very rapidly, in philosophical or general terms, and they are constantly reaching out to "connect" with others. Yellows are such free spirits they tend to change from high to low moods very quickly. Yellows are very social and tend to view life as it ideally should be. They are very emotional, free thinking, and people oriented. Yellow corresponds to the expanding ray of sunshine.

Blue

Blue reflects a "turning down" of autonomic nervous system functions. People who prefer it are more content, calm, and orderly in their speech and body movements. They are very supportive, good listeners, gregarious, and family oriented. Blues do not strive for control. They are more traditional and are preservers of the status quo.

The visual chart depicts blues as contented people who are unconcerned with changing fads, have soft speech, are happy-go-lucky, and are fairly noncompetitive. Blues are very down to earth, seek harmony, and do not like leadership positions. Blue represents the calm of water.

Green

Green is a darker calming color but has more rigidity and less compromise than blue. People who prefer green tend to be independent, self-determining, authority oriented, and are concerned with impressing others with material things. They are task oriented and like security within structured environments. They follow rules and regulations to the letter and do not enjoy being placed in an unfamiliar environment. Greens are very concerned with self-improvement and personal responsibility. They are strong leaders and run their lives by rules and regulations. Green represents the strength of the sequoia tree.

As an exercise, have friends write down their favorite primary color and their least favorite color. Cover up the color headings on Charts V and VI and ask them to place check marks beside those personality characteristics that best represent them. Then add up these characteristics for each column red, yellow, blue, and green. By adding the check marks, you basically can decide their primary color personality type.

Compare this to the colors they listed. By using this procedure with males, females, and persons who represent a cross-section of different socio-economic areas, you will quickly learn the system and at the same time gain many new insights. Sometimes color preference (psychological needs) and the group selected are different as a result of various discrepancies. One of these is the difference between what a person wants to be and what he actually is. As your proficiency increases you will be able to see these personality differences. When you have practiced this procedure with ten or twenty people, you will find yourself making automatic assessments within seconds of new encounters. At this point you will have moved the usual twenty- to thirty-second visual assessment from a subconscious to a conscious level, which you can then use during your next voir dire.

When you have gained further experience, the next step will be to evaluate primary and back-up styles. For example, you will see someone as a blue-red or a yellow-red. Remember, like any behavioral assessment, your accuracy depends upon your level of understanding. After a few months of practice you undoubtedly will be surprised at how much better you understand people.

Color psychology has been a proven aid to medical and psychological diagnosis. When combined with increased knowledge of visual communications and body language, it can become a powerful adjunct to the process of voir dire. Furthermore, the visual communication knowledge covered in this test can help you evaluate your own level of excellence in visual communications and can assist you in your weaker areas.

Chart V

RASICOT'S VISUALLY CODED PERSONALITY TYPES

	RED (16%)	YELLOW (8%)
TENDENCIES	Dominant Competitive Task Oriented Direct Individualist Extrovert Unemotional Lack of Detail Short Attention Span	Flexible Fun Loving People Oriented Creative Social Extrovert Ruled by Emotions Overly Optimistic Philosophical
ENVIRONMENT	New Personal Challenges, Power and Authority	New Group Challenges, Democratic
SPECIALTY	Controlling	Socializing
DRESS	Informal, Casual, Loud, Athletic	Fashionable, Wild, Artistic
JEWELRY	None, Functional	Abundant, Artistic, Unique
BODY LANGUAGE	Expansive, Aggressive, Short Attention Span	Expansive, Friendly
SPEECH	Loud, Harsh, "I" Oriented, Direct	Fast, "We" Oriented
FAVORITE COLOR	Red**	Yellow**

*Percentage of 600 random interviews on subject of favorite color
**6 percent of participants did not answer this question

Chart VI

RASICOT'S VISUALLY CODED PERSONALITY TYPES

	BLUE (58%)	GREEN (12%)
TENDENCIES	Traditional	Orderly
	Conformer	Resist Change
	Follower	Serious
	Loyal	Critical
	Introvert	Introvert
	Group Oriented	Individualist
	Nonleader	Unemotional
	Status Quo	Very Structured
		Uncompromising
ENVIRONMENT	Group Identity	High Status
	Nonleader	Authority
SPECIALTY	Supportive	Technical
DRESS	Casual, Out of Style	Formal, Power Subdued
JEWELRY	Traditional, Family Oriented	Sophisticated Expensive
BODY LANGUAGE	Concentric Nonaggresive	Concentric Aggressive
SPEECH	Soft, Slow, "We" Oriented	Slow, Precise, "I" Oriented
FAVORITE COLOR	Blue**	Green**

*Percentage of 600 random interviews on subject of favorite color
**6 percent of participants did not answer this question

RED - MALE
4.1a - See Chart V

RED - FEMALE
4.1b - See Chart V

161

YELLOW - MALE
4.2a - See Chart V

YELLOW - FEMALE
4.2b - See Chart V

BLUE - MALE
4.3a - See Chart VI

BLUE - FEMALE
4.3b - See Chart VI

163

GREEN - MALE
4.4a - See Chart VI

GREEN - FEMALE
4.4b - See Chart VI

Chart VII

GENERAL JURY CHARACTERISTICS IN CIVIL CASES

PLAINTIF

Blues - Give money most often
    but smaller amoutns

DEFENDANT

Greens - Give least amount of money
    and best chance for no award

GENERAL JURY CHARACTERISTICS IN CRIMINAL CASES

CONVICTION

Identifies with Victim
  Small Families
  Strong Jury Leader
  Pro-Establishment
  Television Viewer
  Pro-Business Orientation
  Blues and Greens

AQUITTAL

Identifies with Defendant
  Large Families
  Leaderless
  Anti-Establishment
  Reader
  Finds Defendant Attractive
  Reds and Yellows

JURY COLOR COMBINATIONS

	PERSONALITY ORIENTATION		SOCIAL ORIENTATION
Green - Self-Respect Blue - Self-Moderation	=	(Serious)	= (Justice)
Yellow - Self Development Red - Self-Confidence	=	(Volatile)	= (Open-Minded)
Red - Self-Confidence Green - Self-Respect	=	(Self-Assured)	= (Responsible)
Yellow - Self-Development Blue - Self-Modertion	=	(Carefree)	= (Tolerant)
Green - Self-Respect Yellow - Self-Development	=	(Self-Reliant)	= (Sincere)
Blue - Self-Moderation Red - Self-Confidence	=	(Confident)	= (Benevolent)

Chart VIII

COLOR PERSONALITY WHEEL

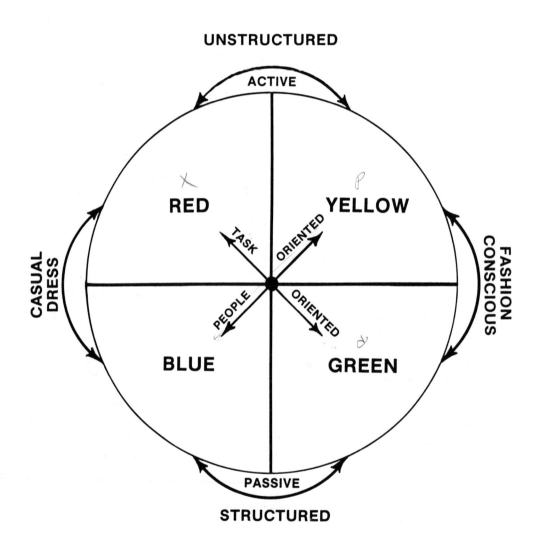

Chart IX

GENERAL PERSONALITY TRAITS

RED
Hot Button: Psychological (Self) Needs
Basic Motive: Personal Independence

TENDENCIES: Dominant
Competitive
Task Oriented
Direct
Individualist
Extrovert

ENVIRONMENT: New Personal
Challenges,
Power and Authority

SPECIALTY: Controlling

PROBLEM: Unemotional, Lack of
Detail, Short
Attention Span

DRESS: Informal, Casual,
Loud, Athletic

BODY LANGUAGE: Aggressive, Dominant,
Short Attention Span

SPEECH: Loud, Harsh, "I"
Oriented, Direct,
I Believe

FAVORITE COLOR: Red

READING: Light reader, short and
concise materials,
Playboy, Sports,
Illustrated, Time

TV SHOWS: Sports, cops and robbers
shows, A-Team, Hill
Street Blues, Miami Vice.
Fast moving, action-
packed shows

HOBBIES: Competitive sports, racing,
tennis, hunting, motor-
cycles

CIVIC INVOLVEMENT: Minimal if any

LEISURE TIME SPENT IN: Competing, conquering

CONGRUENT OCCUPATIONS: Entrepreneurs
Outside Sales People
Commissioned Workers
Real Estate Agents
Used Car Salesman
Athletes
Bartenders
Bouncers
Cab Drivers
Construction Workers

Chart IX (continued)

GENERAL PERSONALITY TRAITS

YELLOW
Hot Button: Sociological (Group) Needs
Basic Motive: Socially Creative

TENDENCIES: Flexible
Fun Loving
People Oriented
Creative
Social
Extrovert

ENVIRONMENT: New Group Challenges,
Democratic

SPECIALTY: Socializing

DRESS: Fahionable, Wild,
Artistic

JEWELRY: Abundant, Artistic,
Unique

BODY LANGUAGE: Expansive, Friendly

SPEECH: Fast, "We" Oriented,
I see, I imagine

FAVORITE COLOR: Yellow

PROBLEM: Ruled by Emotions,
Overly Optimistic,
Philosophical

READING: Long novels,
romantic literature,
fiction. Reads for
pleasure and fantasy.
Gone With the Wind,
People Magazine

TV SHOWS: Dallas, Dynasty,
science fiction,
Star Trek

HOBBIES: Social sports,
volleyball, painting,
writing, reading,
traveling, decorating

CIVIC INVOLVEMENT: Highly involved in
many clubs, theater,
music

LEISURE TIME SPENT IN: New experiences

CONGRUENT OCCUPATIONS: Interior Designers
Musicians
Writers
Photographers
Beauticians
Travel Agents
Receptionists
Advertising
Social Scientists
Artistic People

Chart IX (continued)

GENERAL PERSONALITY TRAITS

BLUE
Hot Button: Sociological (Group) Needs
Basic Motive: Supportive

TENDENCIES: Traditional, Conformer, Follower, Loyal, Group Oriented, Introvert	**READING:** Short stories, condensed novels, local newspapers, Readers Digest, Better Homes & Gardens. Reads to fill time
ENVIRONMENT: Group Identity, Nonleader	**TV SHOWS:** Situation comedies, soap operas, All in the Family, Alice, Cosby Show
SPECIALTY: Supportive	
DRESS: Casual, Out of Style, Subdued	**HOBBIES:** Family trips, camping, fishing, Boy Scouts
JEWELRY: Traditional, Family	**CIVIC INVOLVEMENT:** Highly involved, PTA, humane society, fund raisers
BODY LANGUAGE: Concentric, Nonaggressive	
SPEECH: Soft, Slow, "We" Oriented, I Feel	**LEISURE TIME SPENT IN:** Group involvement
FAVORITE COLOR: Blue	**CONGRUENT OCCUPATIONS:** Counselors, Secretaries, Housewives, Elementary Teachers, Nurses, Farmers, Clerks, Union Members, Waitresses, Factory Workers
PROBLEM: Nonleader, Compromising	

Chart IX (continued)

GENERAL PERSONALITY TRAITS

GREEN
Hot Button: Psychological (Self) Needs
Basic Motive: Social Power

TENDENCIES:	Orderly Resist Change Serious Critical Individualist Introvert
ENVIRONMENT:	High Status, Authority
SPECIALTY:	Technical
DRESS:	Formal, Power
JEWELRY:	Sophisticated, Expensive
SPEECH:	Slow, Precise, "I" Oriented, I think
FAVORITE COLOR:	Green
PROBLEM:	Unemotional, Too Factual, Uncompromising
READING:	Heavy reader on self-help materials, nonfiction, technical, reads for knowledge. Wall Street Journal, Business Week, national newspapers
TV SHOWS:	Documentaries, historical educational TV, 20/20, 60 Minutes, news
HOBBIES:	Individualized collecting, stamps, cars, antiques, art
CIVIC INVOLVEMENT:	Very selective, club officer, rotary club, school board, city council
LEISURE TIME SPENT IN:	Self-improvement
CONGRUENT OCCUPATIONS:	Lawyers Engineers Doctors Accountants Computer Programmers Editors Military Officers Ministers College Professors

Chart X

ALL BEHAVIOR FULFILLS SOME NEED

THREE TYPES OF NEEDS

1. PHYSIOLOGICAL (PHYSICAL)— Food, water, shelter
2. PSYCHOLOGICAL (MENTAL)— Ego, Self-Esteem, Our Beliefs
3. SOCIOLOGICAL (SOCIAL) — Group Acceptance, Society's Beliefs

EXAMPLES

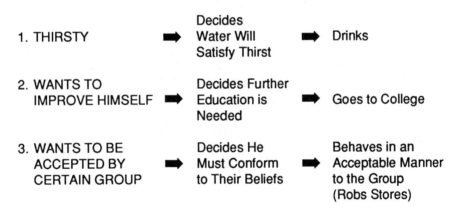

When jurors or witnesses act a certain way a red light should go off in your head signaling the thought "Why did they want to express themselves that way?" and "What did they get out of it?" The more you understand about human needs and behavior the better equipped you are to persuade other people to your side.

JURY'S NEEDS

1. PHYSICAL—To be comfortable; lighting, temperature, seating

2. MENTAL—A need to feel important, to be fair to oneself

3. SOCIAL—To be accepted by the group, to be fair to society

EXAMPLES

1. Juror wants to end deliberation because ➡ of her physical discomfort | She decides she can go home earlier if she ends the deadlock and sides with the majority. ➡ | She agrees with the majority.

2. Juror has very strong personal beliefs about this case and ➡ she must be true to herself. | Even though her beliefs conflict with the rest of the jury and the testimony, she feels she is right. ➡ | She stays with her beliefs and will not be influenced by the pressure from the group.

3. Juror feels a responsibility to society and the group. ➡ | Even though her beliefs conflict with the group she feels the group must be right and she must fit in. ➡ | She votes with the group and suppresses her personal feelings

In the preceding examples, juror #1 voted to satisfy her physical needs. Juror #2 voted to satisfy her needs and suppressed her social needs. Juror #3 voted to satisfy her social needs and suppressed her mental needs.

Human behavior is influenced by a combination of all three types of needs. When two or more needs are in conflict, however, the person's dominant needs will prevail. The lawyer who fulfills the most needs for each juror will win.

VOIR DIRE QUESTIONS

When it comes time to draft your voir dire questions you will find it helpful to organize your thoughts into two basic groups: (1) individual questions, and (2) group questions. Your goal should be to cover all eight subject matters explained below.

EIGHT AREAS OF QUESTIONING

The eight areas of questioning you want to cover in your voir dire are (1) introduction, (2) occupation, (3) education, (4) family, (5) spare time, (6) legal experience, (7) relevant issues, and (8) final exit questions. These eight areas should be covered in all civil and criminal cases.

In the introduction you want a smooth way to start your questioning, you want to introduce yourself and your client, and you want to relax the jury panel. The important things to include in your short (two minute) introduction are (1) reintroduce yourself and your client; (2) tell the jury the nature of the case and as much brief information about the case as your rules allow; (3) explain the reason for your questioning: you are strangers and need to get acquainted; (4) explain that justice requires truthfulness from everyone, including the jury; and (5) explain that there are no right or wrong answers to your questions; you are asking about their thoughts and feelings.

INDIVIDUAL QUESTIONS

The individual questions you should ask the prospective jurors include occupation, education, family, and spare time. Some of this information you may already have from the jury questionnaires, the judge's questions, or the plaintiff/prosecutor's questions. If you do not have the information from these sources you should cover these areas.

The questions on occupation will tell you what the jurors have elected to do for eight hours each working day. You also find out if their jobs are people oriented (teacher, sales, cab driver) or product oriented (computer programmer, accountant, mechanic). The two important things to discover about the jurors' occupations are what do they do now and what were their previous occupations.

The jurors' education will give you a clue about whether or not they have had special training in the relevant areas of your case, whether or not they can follow a line of reasoning, whether or not they can complete a long-term goal, and their degree of establishmentism.

The family questions will show you trends in upbringing, similar or dissimilar life styles, and attitudes on children. Two things you need to look for are spouse/family member occupation and spouse/family member education.

What somebody elects to do in his spare time tells you something about that person. Does that person have hobbies, belong to clubs or organizations, do volunteer work, read, or watch television? The two basic things you are looking for are (1) does the person spend his spare time with himself (stamp collecting, building model airplanes—defense oriented) or does he spend his spare time with groups of people (coaching, PTA, Lion's Club—plaintiff oriented); and (2) are the person's spare time activities benefiting himself only (defense) or are they benefiting others (plaintiff)?

GROUP QUESTIONS

The questions you ask the entire group are designed to elicit information about the prospective jurors' legal experience and feelings about the relevant issues in your case and to smoothly end your questioning.

You want to know who has been a juror before, what kind of case it was (civil or criminal), if anyone has any legal training, and if anyone has ever been involved in a lawsuit or trial. You are basically looking for two things: (1) the jurors' legal knowledge and experience, and (2) their biases or prejudices towards the legal system.

The questions pertaining to relevant issues in your case and the jury's attitudes towards them are the most important and need to be developed very carefully. Depending upon the case, these issues may be related to race, money, punishment, different life styles, fairness, burden of proof, or pain and suffering. Questions in these areas must be perfectly worded or they may result in embarrassment, irritation of the jurors, or false or misleading answers from the jurors. A great deal of thought must be put into these questions in order to achieve your goals.

The final few voir dire exit questions are asked in order to smoothly end your questioning and to end on an "upbeat," positive rapport with the jury. Your final questions could be, for example, "How many of you would do your best to be fair to both sides in this case?" or "How many of you honestly feel you would be a fair juror in this case?"

Obviously, different jurisdictions handle voir dire differently. Some are very liberal, some are extremely conservative, and some fall in between. Regardless of how your jurisdiction handles voir dire, your goal is to find out as much information as possible about each prospective juror while staying within the rules of the court. Sometimes you can get only a small amount of information about the jurors, and sometimes you can get a large amount of information about the jurors, but try to elicit as much information as possible. Your accuracy should increase as your information increases.

SUMMARY

The personal indicators of individuals tell us a great deal about their personalities. We all surround ourselves with clues about our personalities. We surround ourselves with the things with which we are most comfortable (clothing, hair styles, jewelry, friends, jobs). Your understanding of basic personalities is greatly improved when you combine visual indicators with verbal responses. Assessing jurors visually and verbally to determine their primary personality types provides much additional information about who will potentially harm your case the most, who the foreperson is likely to be, and how best to gain rapport and credibility with individual jurors.

In chapter 5 I will review the form, strategies, and timing of the opening statement.

Chapter **5**

OPENING
STATEMENT

This case is about:

no more than 4 statements

(sentences)

INTRODUCTION

Contemporary Americans are the most visually oriented people in our history. Newspaper readership has steadily fallen as American dependence on visual media continues to increase. Our general reliance on "visuals" rather than "verbals" necessitates new strategies in the courtroom and the need to increase familiarity with visual technology. The problem: jurors are visually oriented and trials are verbally oriented. Visual aids can clearly assist in bridging the gap between the two basic orientations. It is equally important to understand how and when to use these aids effectively. If the climax comes in the beginning of the trial, what follows may be interpreted as dull and uninteresting.

In addition to the use of visual aids in the courtroom, you will be continually evaluated on those other components of your nonverbal image previously discussed: space usage, timing or pacing, demeanor, image and dress, and speech. The following paragraphs will outline those major aspects of the visual trial that will increase your effectiveness as a communicator during opening statement.

FORM

You should paint a clear picture of exactly what you are going to do and how you are going to do it. When you have completed your opening comments, jurors should know basically what the case is about, how you will prove your position, and what you are asking of them. The opening statement should be organized around three or four main issues that you want the jury to remember throughout the trial.

Opening statements should be no longer than twenty minutes. After twenty minutes the memory recall curve drops significantly. Television executives have used this principle for years in deciding when to insert commercials during a program. After a twenty- to thirty-minute cycle, some change should occur, and then you can recycle into another twenty- to thirty-minute segment. If you cannot give a meaningful twenty-minute opening statement, you might want to reconsider your central theme to determine if it is correctly focused. Specific names, dates, places, and other facts will be elaborated upon during the case-in-chief, so the opening statement should be spent summarizing your case.

It is effective to use a simple outline on the blackboard during opening statement to show the organization of your position (5.1a) and (5. 1b). Unfortunately some judges do not allow blackboards and other visual aids during opening statements. If the court's goal is to facilitate communication, this position is counterproductive. Complicated technical cases frequently employ esoteric terminology. Jurors cannot be expected to digest overwhelming, intricate word pictures. Not permitting attorneys to use models, charts, or blackboards during opening statements restricts communication as much as insisting that veniremen be questioned in a "dark room." All visual aids used during an opening statement should, of course, be discussed in chambers before the trial to eliminate any confusion or legal misunderstanding.

Visual aids should be used whenever possible. They accomplish two goals: (1) they aid understanding, and (2) they add interest, which extends the jury's attention span.

HALO EFFECT

Preconditioning the jury to the positive essentials of your case creates what is called the "halo effect." The "halo effect" means that you have a strong tendency to see what you want to see and hear what you want to hear. Psychologically, people mold new information into what they want it to be. When you expect something to be good, you tend to look for the positive points that reinforce your initial impressions and to disregard most negative points. Conversely, if you expect a negative experience, you will tend to be very critical about the event.

OPENING STATEMENT

I. DEFENDANT WAS DRIVING
  A. SPEEDING
  B. VEHICLE SLID OUT OF CONTROL
  C. REAR ENDED JOHN
II. COLLISION CAUSED INJURIES
  A. BROKEN BACK
  B. PARALYZED
  C. BRAIN DAMAGE
III. DAMAGES
  A. PAST
  B. FUTURE
  C. PAIN, SUFFERING

5.1a • Clear and Precise Outline

5.1b • Disorganized and Distracting

PRIMACY AND RECENCY

Primacy means that the facts you believe first will have the most influence on your interpretation of future facts. *Recency* means that the last facts you hear are remembered the best. The longer and more intricate your arguments become the more important are the principles of primacy and recency. When you organize your case around three or four key points and mention them both at the beginning of your opening statement and at the end, you have used both principles to good psychological advantage. When key points are reinforced throughout the opening statement, jurors will tend to remember them in much the same fashion as they would a catchy radio commercial: the tune will be mentally whistled long after the commercial has ended.

Primacy is of paramount importance in your opening statement. After the jurors have heard both opening statements they have, in lay terms, heard "both side of the story." After hearing "both sides of the story" they will then lean subconsciously towards one side. Once they lean towards one side they generally begin to view the rest of the trial from that perspective because it reinforces their initial judgment.

SIX "DO'S" OF OPENING STATEMENT

1. Speak plain English
2. Be brief and concise
3. Summarize the main ideas
4. Understate rather than overstate
5. Use positive language
6. Continue to gain positive rapport

SIX "DON'TS" OF OPENING STATEMENT

If the pace and structure of opening statements is to build to a synchronized climax, you do not have time for:

1. The extensive use of technical jargon that demands definition. If technical jargon is used without definition, communication blockage is a foregone conclusion. Use your witnesses to explain the details.
2. Civic lectures on the merits of American jurisprudence.
3. A demonstration of your IQ or individual war stories.
4. Elaborate word pictures substituted for visual aids.
5. Flowery elaborations and wordy explanations.
6. The reading of a technically worded statement. Additionally, reading from your written notes will reduce rapport with jurors and make it very difficult to "read" their nonverbal responses. If you cannot give an opening statement without extensive notes (a skeleton outline is fine), it means one of three things: (1) you are not familiar enough with your case; (2) you have not focused your case properly; or (3) your opening statement is much too technical.

SPACE

When you are permitted to move freely about the courtroom, territorial and social space become major considerations. The jury box will begin to be claimed by individual jurors by the time the opening statements are given. Remember, six to eight feet is a safe distance from the jury. If you are farther away than eight feet, you will lose involvement. If you are closer than six feet, you may make the jury uncomfortable.

It may be helpful to visualize yourself surrounded by a bubble of social space. Courtesy for the space bubble of others is programmed into our cultural norms. Consideration for the social and territorial space of others is one of the nonverbal indicators that jurors will use to evaluate you in terms of fairness and social etiquette. Social space is important in terms of how you use it for gesturing, standing, sitting, and movement. The lower plane of vertical space is where you soften your gestures and tone down your movements. The upper plane is used for dramatic effect and emphasis.

DEMEANOR

A person's demeanor typically represents 60 percent of the total message communicated to others. Demeanor that reflects double messages destroys the courtroom attorney's credibility. As a precaution, present your opening and closing statements to a third party and have her critique your presentation. It is also a desirable practice to give your opening and closing statements to someone who is unfamiliar with legal terminology: someone much like the jurors who will be evaluating these same words.

Overall courtroom demeanor should be assessed in terms of the major social values you want others to associate with you as a professional. You want to be seen as an expert, as a possessor of a keen sense of fairness, and as an individual who believes in the equality of humankind. If these general characteristics are not part of your overall demeanor, you have lost professional credibility and have unnecessarily created psychological distance between you and the jurors whom you want to identify with your case.

Remember, gestures and movement add interest to a speech. When a speaker is standing behind a podium the speech becomes very boring very quickly. Podiums are a security blanket for the speaker but a blocking distraction for the listener. If you are in federal court and are required to speak from the podium, stand to the side of it so the jury sees more than just a talking head.

OVERALL IMAGE

Your professional courtroom image is interlinked with all five areas of personal assessment that have been discussed in this text. You are assessed both individually and as part of the total team. Much like a football game, the drama of the courtroom pits one team against another. Any member of the team who does not fit the overall image is giving out contradictory signals.

WORDS

A common language error used by lawyers is overuse of the expression "evidence will show." This phrase depersonalizes the facts or information that follow and is equivalent to neglecting to use jurors' names during voir dire. If you addressed jury members only as "officers of the court" or veniremen, the psychological effect would be similar to overuse of the statement "evidence will show." Psychological identification is facilitated with the use of names and first-person references. "We will prove" or "we will show you" are more personal statements. You are promising the jury you will prove your case, and your opening will assist the jury in organizing the proof.

Sarcasm requires you to demean qualities of another; it is a form of put down. To demean another you must put yourself in a superior position. You never know who will associate himself with the object of the put down and feel personally slighted even though the comment was not directed at him.

Humor plays with the normative edge of what is socially proper or improper. Ethnic jokes put down one group of people at the expense of another. Humor always represents value and attitude differences between people. To use humor with any frequency is to systematically violate the individual values of some persons. Humor should therefore be used very carefully if at all. The jurors are all strangers to you and they all have different values and different senses of humor. It is true that humor generally relaxes people. But your ultimate goal is not to have the jury believe you are a talented comic but to have them believe you are a serious-minded lawyer fighting for justice.

REASONS TO RESERVE OPENING STATEMENTS

There are five major reasons you, as defense counsel, may choose not to give an opening statement until the beginning of your case:

1. A wish to conceal your overall strategy or theory from the opposing side.
2. To affect a passive posture in order to be open to any theory that might arise during your adversaries' case.
3. The adversaries' evidence is so forceful or damaging that your "thunder" would be preempted through early disclosure.
4. To force your adversaries to prove many side issues they normally wouldn't try to prove because they aren't sure which areas of their case you will be attacking.
5. To differentiate yourself from the other defendants in a multi-defendant case if the other defendants' opening statements tell the story.

Obviously, the risk of reserving your opening statement is that the jurors may make up their minds before you even begin your case. They may assume that you don't have a rebuttal to your adversary's theory. This idea can be neutralized during voir dire if done carefully. Reserving an opening statement is a very risky move, and I recommend it only in about one out of every one hundred cases.

SUMMARY

Opening statements will strongly influence the interpretations jurors will give to subsequent information covered throughout the remainder of the trial. The three or four main points of your case should be totally understood by the jury upon completion of the opening argument. Defense counsel may wish to consider the positive and negative aspects of withholding opening statement in unique cases. The four important things to remember about opening statements are: (1) this is the first time the jurors have heard your side of the story and it is your responsibility to make them understand the facts; (2) what the jurors believe after opening statements will influence how they view the evidence throughout the trial; (3) the jury needs to know your position in very specific terms; and (4) the jury needs guidance concerning the important issues to watch for during the trial.

Chapter 6 will demonstrate effective and ineffective methods of physically presenting evidence.

DEMONSTRATIVE EVIDENCE AND THE JURY'S VIEW

INTRODUCTION

The effect that evidence has on the jury can be enhanced or diminished by how it is presented. My primary focus in this chapter is to illustrate the impact that visual evidence has on the jury.

DEMONSTRATIVE EVIDENCE

When you are planning your trail strategy, the five most important things to decide about demonstrative evidence are: (1) what parts of the case can be enhanced by visual support; (2) what kind of visual support will be most effective; (3) where in the courtroom should you display the visual support; (4) during what stage of the trial do you want the visual evidence shown; and (5) how sophisticated should the visual evidence be for this case and this jury.

Demonstrative evidence is generally best presented as soon as possible during the first part of the trial. It can then be referred to during the entire case-in-chief and used as a refresher during closing argument.

WEAPONS

How and where you hold evidence is very important. You increase the threatening or aggressive qualities of weapons by holding them in the upper vertical plane and holding them in a ready-to-use position. Illustration (6.1a) emphasizes the threatening effect and illustration (6.1b) decreases the threatening effect. Movements in the upper vertical plane possess more force and power than those in the lower plane.

Repeating the same procedure with the knife in illustrations (6.2a) and (6.2b) you observe the same difference in effect. The important point is to visualize the effect from the jury's point of view. The effect of weapons on jurors changes as spatial distances are adjusted.

WEAPONS—GUN

6.1a
• Threatening
• Dramatic
• Upper Plane
• Ready to Use

6.1b
• Nonthreatening
• Undramatic
• Lower Plane
• Handled Loosely
• Partially Covered

WEAPONS—KNIFE

6.2a
- Threatening
- Upper Plane
- Broad Side Showing
- Ready to Use

6.2b
- Nonthreatening
- Lower Plane
- Narrow Side Showing
- Relaxed Grip

A knife blade displayed showing the wide flat side is more awesome than a narrow side view of the cutting edge. The more carefully you hold a weapon the more dangerous it appears, or you can lessen the weapon's force by the opposite handling procedures. These techniques will help the jury "feel" the impact of evidence. The more senses the jurors use to interpret facts the more involved they become and the greater the psychological impact of those facts.

The same visual effects hold true for handling evidence in civil cases such as products liability trials.

CHARTS AND BLACKBOARDS

A picture is worth a thousand words. In illustrations (6.3a) and (6.3b) I have presented a diagram of an intersection from the jury's perspective. In (6.3a) the visual impact is greater than in (6.3b). The jurors view objects at a distance more impartially than those closer to their innermost spacial zones. If necessary, you should have a moveable demonstration stand available in order to gain the maximum desired effect. Basically, the impact of any demonstrative evidence decreases as spatial distance increases.

Whenever it is possible to get jury members to handle evidence, photographs, weapons, models, or replicas, the impact increases because three senses are used. They are hearing about it, they see it, and they feel it.

A common courtroom mistake is to use your body inadvertently as a blocking device, which lessens your visual aid's impact. In illustration (6.4a) the attorney has positioned himself correctly while using the blackboard. Conversely, in illustration (6.4b) he has incorrectly used his body to block part of the evidence. Using your body as a blocking device in this manner is irritating to jurors because it breaks up their concentration.

In illustration (6.4c) counsel is maintaining a relatively open front for the jury. In illustration (6.4d) not only is his body used as a blocking device but he also has squarely presented his back in the most

CHARTS

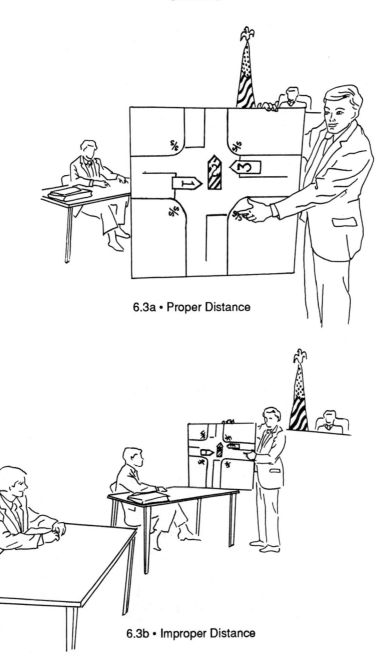

6.3a • Proper Distance

6.3b • Improper Distance

6.4a • Proper Positioning

6.4b • Improper Positioning

unfriendly manner possible. Illustration (6.4d) is not only a turnoff but also creates an image of secrecy.

I have suggested throughout this text that friendliness and identification are enhanced by openness: open front, open palming gestures, as well as language and imagery that permit the jurors to identify with you. Remember, your personal relationship with the jury is very important to your case.

EXHIBITS

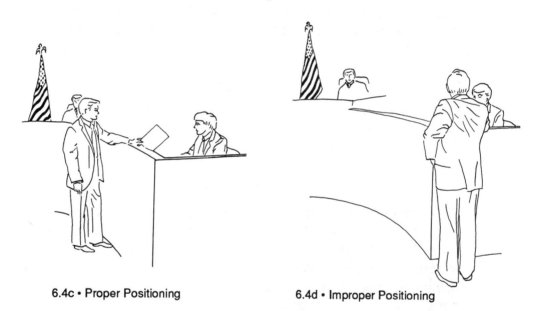

6.4c • Proper Positioning   6.4d • Improper Positioning

PROS AND CONS OF VISUAL AIDS

Using visual aids during a trial is not risk free. You could overuse them, use something that your adversary turns against you, fumble with machines that do not work, use models that break as you are using them, and many other pitfalls. These are some of the reasons why visual aids must be carefully thought out and effectively produced. If your planning eliminates the negative aspects of the visual aid, the overall effectiveness of using visual aids can be tremendous.

It is best to think through the pros and cons of each type of visual aid before you decide which ones you want to use during your trial. Listed below are the pros and cons of the most widely used visual aids.

VISUAL AID

Pros   *Cons*

Blackboards

Readily available; easy to use; wil not malfunction; proceed at your own pace

Can be used by other side; erasable; lost information

Blow-ups

Excellent tool; easy to see; lifelike; will not malfunction; easy to revise; show entire jury

Cost

Flip Charts

Excellent tool; easy to follow; keeps jury's attention; effectively revised during closing; easily folded up so opponent cannot use it; use black, green, blue, and red pens; can be spontaneously written on during testimony or preproduced at your leisure; inexpensive

Sometimes cumbersome; do not overuse; main points only

Video

Adds interest with movement; jury sees live action; shows jury things that cannot be brought into courtroom (scenes, buildings, machinery)

Proceeds at an uniterrupted, constant pace; needs special equipment and lighting; possible mechanical problems; after viewing, the information is locked in cassette; cost

Pros	Cons

Models

Jury can see and feel the product or idea	Possible malfunction; cost

Overhead Projectors

Easy to enlarge scene or item; proceed at your own pace	Usually poor lighting; needs screen or blank wall; cumbersome to use; possible mechanical problems; cost

Slides

Jury sees real things; proceed at your own pace	Lights must be adjusted; needs screen; possible mechanical problems; cost

SURVIVAL KIT

Demonstrative evidence can be extremely beneficial if presented at the right time and with the right emphasis. Practice using the equipment before the trial so you do not lose the impact by fumbling through the presentation. I recommend a survival kit of odds and ends be kept in your briefcase for unplanned problems. The kit should include extra pens and pencils, an extra projector bulb, felt-tip pens for flip charts (if the cap is "accidently left off the pen" when your adversary is finished, the pen may be dried out when you begin to present your case), scotch tape, extension cord, and band-aids.

Be prepared for any breakup in your prepared flow of the case. A very positive image is projected when your adversary needs an extension cord or a light bulb and you give him the equipment he needs in order to continue. The same image is created if someone is bruised or cut accidently in the courtroom or hallway and you offer temporary assistance. You may never need the items in this kit, but the effect, if you do need them, is tremendous.

COURTROOM SEATING

Unless your client has an appearance that is particularly distracting, you will want to increase your client's exposure by sitting him or her at the table nearest to the jury. If the client is especially attractive, research indicates that jurors will increase their identification and liking. Verdicts and awards tend to be more favorable when clients have an appealing image.

In illustration (6.5a) counsel has decided to decrease the jury's view of his client by occupying the seat nearest to the jury. In illustration (6.5b) the female client is given maximum exposure. The more open, warm, and personable clients can be made to appear the better your chances for a favorable verdict.

When a client is totally visible he or she must be careful to observe good posture and personal habits throughout the trial. Clothing should be appropriately neat and compatible with your team's image and strategy.

In illustration (6.5c) the woman has used her body as a blocking device, from the perspective of the jury, and has created the impression of secrecy. The open form of consultations is presented in illustration (6.5d). A way to think of your visual image in the courtroom is to adopt a jury-centered perspective. In a fashion similar to actors on a stage, you are constantly "playing to the audience."

Remember, someone on the jury is watching you and your client at all times.

COURTROOM SEATING

6.5a • Minimum Client Exposure

6.5b • Maximum Client Exposure

CONSULTATION

6.5c
• Closed
• Secretive

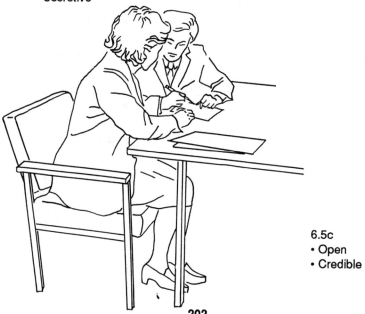

6.5c
• Open
• Credible

SUMMARY

How, where, and when evidence is presented significantly determines the impact it will have on jurors. American culture is highly visually oriented. When you appeal to this visual orientation, jurors tend to become more interested and involved. I cannot stress enough how the proper use of visual aids can dramatically add interest and understanding to your case.

Chapter 7 will discuss the form, strategy, and manner of presentation for closing arguments.

CLOSING STATEMENTS

INTRODUCTION

Rules for final argument are not well defined and do not prevent "advocacy" in the sense of open persuasion. Your ability to persuade in final argument will depend to a large extent on the image you have already established with the jurors. It is difficult to win a case in final argument; but I have seen many cases lost in final argument.

How well you have integrated the verbal and visual trials will dramatically affect your ability to persuade the jury during final argument. If diagrams and visual aids were orchestrated throughout the trial, key points will have been reinforced and imprinted on the minds of the jurors. Notes taken by jurors should highlight the key points that have been verbally and visually coordinated.

Your closing statement should be organized in the same form as your opening statement, but more time should be spent on reminding the jury which witnesses and evidence proved each of your three main points. Subjective awards should be "seeded" with a high and a low figure instead of one specific amount. When one amount is given to the jurors, their natural reaction is to question it because of a defensive reaction to being ordered to do something. When high/low figures are given, you give them the opportunity to decide what they consider fair. You will then eliminate their initial defensive reaction. You have planted a range from which they probably will decide on a midrange figure. So, if you are the plaintiff and expect $50,000, your range should be from $50,000 to $95,000. If you are the defense in the same case, your range should be from $10,000 to $50,000. In either case, if you can persuade the jurors to your side and they compromise on your reward, you are money ahead.

All of the proper communication techniques that have been discussed through this book should be used during closing argument. This chapter is not shorter because closing argument is less important than other parts of the trial but because I have already discussed and illustrated the effective relevant trial techniques.

EIGHT "DO'S" OF CLOSING STATEMENTS

1. Present an overall image of being positive, serious, and credible.
2. Summarize how you have proven each of your main points by using the same outline as you presented in your opening statement.
3. Explain what you want the jurors to do and give them the reason for doing it.
4. Make the interrogatory questions easy for the jurors to answer. Take all the work out of any mathematical ideas.
5. If you have gained positive rapport, space zones are now more flexible and gesturing can be more aggressive. This is because of your evolution from a "nonperson" lawyer to a "social friend."
6. Time used to deliver your final argument, in most cases, still should be the twenty- to thirty-minute rule that was discussed earlier. If the trial was long and technical, jurors will be listening with one ear; therefore, it is even more important that you be as focused and concise as possible. Only the major weaknesses of your opponent's case along with the main strengths of yours should be covered. The rule in closing statements is that after thirty minutes, unless you make it very interesting, the jury is either in the neutral mode or the negative mode.
7. Graphic terminology representing your position has been used and reinforced throughout the trial, and now is your chance to get the most out of these words. For example, the plaintiff's side will use terms such as *collision* and *pain,* while the defense will strive for the opposite effect with the terms *accident* and *discomfort.*
8. In civil cases basic money sums should have been introduced at the beginning of the trial. Elevating a juror's thinking level for large set-tlements requires repeated reinforcement, and final dollar sums should not be left to the jury's imagination unless you have very low special damages and are hoping for a high pain and suffering award. A breakdown of the basic damage categories needs to be visually displayed when at all possible, but most summary totals should be presented by the plaintiff. As a plaintiff, you want to give

the jurors the sum figure for past expenses and the sum figure for future expenses and have them spend the majority of their time debating the question of pain and suffering. You can mold them into this pattern by the way you present your damage claims. As a defendant, you want the jurors to justify each and every little expense, and you may attempt to pick on a few questionable charges to program them to audit all of the claims. The more bills they discuss, the better your chances of a lower award.

Pain and suffering is the one category from which money is most difficult to recover because it is something the jury cannot see or feel. Your job as a plaintiff's attorney is to get the jurors to feel vicariously your client's pain and suffering. At the end of the trial, if the jury does not have personal empathy for the plaintiff, it is very difficult to receive large damages over and above the actual special damages. In plaintiff cases it is generally much easier to get large damages from an angry or a loving jury than it is from a logical, driven jury. Remember, people make decisions through emotions first, and then those emotions guide their logic.

A specific breakdown of pain and suffering dollar value is needed to give jurors a logical reason to make the award. Explain that $10 a day for pain and suffering is $3,650 a year and your client's life expectancy is twenty years, which equals $73,000. If they think your client's pain and suffering is worth $30 a day, that is $10,950 a year, which is $219,000 over her lifetime. What they should decide is how much her pain and suffering is worth per day. Two hundred nineteen thousand dollars scares some people, but the difference between $10 and $30 is not enough to argue about. The defense conversely attacks the large inflationary figures. Notice how in pain and suffering (emotional damages) the defendant and plaintiff reverse positions regarding sum versus individual costs.

FOUR "DON'TS" OF CLOSING STATEMENTS

1. Don't read a closing statement. This is the time you need all the rapport you have earned throughout the trial
2. Don't use humor. You want the jurors to believe in your credibility and believe in the seriousness of their decision.
3. Don't beg. Don't use phrases like "if you can see it in your heart." You are there for justice, not sympathy. Sympathy implies you did not prove your position and now you want the jury to decide on emotions (which both attorneys and the judge have spoken against during the trial).
4. Don't use sarcasm or put downs against the other team. Mudslinging has a negative effect and implies a position of weakness.

FORM

The form of your closing argument is basically the same as your opening statement, but now you can explain how you have proven each point. (7.1a)

7.1 • Closing Statement

SUMMARY

Although it is almost impossible to win a case solely by a good closing argument, it is possible to lose a case with a poor closing argument. The closing argument provides the jurors with support for the opinions they have already formed.

Your closing statement should contain the same outline and key points as you presented in your opening statement and throughout your case-in-chief. At the time of the closing argument, however, the jurors can be specifically shown how you have proven your case and why they should return a verdict for your position.

FINAL THOUGHTS

Successful trial attorneys understand the two basic problems they are confronted with in every case: (1) The legal workup of the case, and (2) the presentation of the case to a judge or a jury. Neither the legal workup nor the presentation of the case can stand alone. Both aspects must be effectively integrated to achieve a successful result. Presenting a strong legal case in a confusing manner is as unproductive as dynamically presenting a weak case. This book is directed towards the second problem: effectively communicating the case to the jury.

Verdicts are normally decided by assessing both verbal and nonverbal information that is presented throughout the trial. Human decisions are made by combining emotions with facts. Emotions come first; facts come second. Emotions function as a filter, excluding or enhancing certain facts. Research has shown that, given the same set of facts, jurors will give more money to people they like than to people they dislike. Jurors will convict an unattractive defendant more often than an attractive defendant.

Every trial attorney knows that credibility and positive rapport with the jury are very important. Positive rapport and credibility are assessed by conscious and subconscious interpretations. Rapport and credibility are basically determined by assessing five interrelated areas: (1) appearance, (2) body language, (3) space usage, (4) time usage, and (5) verbal skills. As violations in these areas increase, the likelihood of negative rapport increases. When attorneys or witnesses are negatively perceived, their powers of persuasion are substantially reduced.

A clear, concise, congruent theme is paramount in presenting a case. The nonverbal images of the attorney, client, and witnesses must support and be consistent with their verbal images. For instance, in determining the appropriate attire for a witness, the trial attorney must ask: (1) What does the witness feel comfortable wearing (suit, sweater, shirt)? (2) What role does the witness play (expert, co-worker, friend, victim)? (3) What type of jury is the witness communicating with (rural, urban, informal, formal)? The dress continuum ranges from very formal (three-piece dark suit, white shirt, foulard tie, plain tie shoes) to very informal (plaid shirt, slacks, loafers). An expert is usually dressed at the formal end of the continuum, while a factory worker is usually dressed at the informal end of the continuum. The dress of attorneys, clients, or witnesses must be consistent with their roles, demeanors, and verbal skills.

In voir dire, the paramount objective is to eliminate the veniremen who appear to be most harmful to your position. A personality profile of unwanted veniremen should be determined before the trial begins. Each voir dire question asked should accomplish one or more of these objectives: (1) elicit information about the venireman, (2) gain positive rapport with the venireman, or (3) covertly plant the seeds for the theme of the case. Verbal responses and nonverbal behavior (dress, demeanor, space usage, time usage) are combined for a total assessment.

One of the principles of the Rasicot Personality System is that every person's appearance and behavior is a conscious and subconscious reflection of his personality. By observing and interpreting the jurors' images, a better understanding of their personalities is attained. Consequently, a more accurate prediction of their behavior occurs. This ability is even more important when voir dire is severely limited. The personality system is ideal for use in federal and state courts in which attorneys cannot question veniremen.

This book focuses on three basic ideas: (1) describing the social rules of how people communicate with each other: verbally and nonverbally; (2) illustrating how to orchestrate a team's image to be consistent with the personalities, the case, and the makeup of the jury; (3) increasing observation and interpretation of personality signs of jurors and witnesses in order to be an effective communicator.

Presenting a case to lay jurors who know nothing about the legal issues and nothing about the legal process can be frustrating. By using sound psychological, sociological, and legal principles throughout the trial, you can improve your trial skills, present a more effective case, and better serve your clients.

Don't pursue perfection, create it!

Trial Consultation

Dr. James Rasicot
6705 Woodedge Road
Minneapolis, Minnesota 55364
(612) 472-4717

BIBLIOGRAPHY

Altman, I., and D. Taylor. *Social Penetration: The Development of Interpersonal Relations*. Holt, Rinehart & Winston, Inc., 1973.

Ashcraft, Norman. *People Space*. Anchor Books, 1976.

Ayres J. "Perceived use of Evaluative Statements in Developing, Stable, and Deteriorating Relationships with a Person of the Same or Opposite Sex." *Western Journal of Speech Communication* 46 (1982): 20-31.

Bell, R.R. *Worlds of Friendship*. Sage, 1981.

Berger, C., and R. Calabrese. "Some Explorations in Initial Interaction and Beyond: Toward a Developmental Theory of Interpersonal Communication." *Human Communication Research* 1 (1975): 99-112.

Berger, C., G. Clatterbuck, R. Gardner, and L. Schulman. "Perceptions of Information Sequencing in Relationship Development." *Human Communication Research* 3 (1976): 29-46.

Bryan, William. J. Jr. *The Chosen Ones: The Psychology of Jury Selection*. Vantage Press, 1971.

_____. *Civil Trial Tactics*. Minnetonka Bar Association, 1983.

Cooper, Ken. *Nonverbal Communications for Business Success*. Amacom, 1979.

Cundiff, Merlyn. *Kinesics The Silent Command*. Park Publishing, 1972.

Dane, Archer. *How to Expand Your S.I.Q. (Social Intelligence Quotient)*. M. Evans and Co., 1980.

Davis, Flora. *Inside Intuition*. New American Library, Inc., 1973.

Davis, M. *Intimate Relations*. The Free Press, 1973.

Dell Humes, ed. *Language in Culture and Society*. Harper and Row, 1964.

Fast, Julius. *The Body Language of Sex, Power, and Aggression*. Jove Publications, 1978.

Goffman, Erving. *Encounters*. Bobbs-Merrill Co., Inc., 1961.

Henley, Nancy M. *Body Politics*. Prentice Hall, Inc., 1977.

Herbert, David L., and Roger K. Barrett. *Attorney's Master Guide to Courtroom Psychology*. Executive Reports Corp., 1981.

_____. *Human Behavior*. April 1979.

Jeans, James W. *Trial Advocacy.* West Publishing Corp., 1977.

Jordan, Walter E. *Jury Selection.* McGraw-Hill, 1980.

Jourard, S. M. *The Transparent Sell.* Van Nostrand, 1964.

Just, Glen A., ed. *Jury Selection and the Visual Trial: A Lecture Series by James F. Rasicot.* William Mitchell Law Publications, 1983.

Kanter, Frederick H., and Arnold P. Goldstein, eds. *Helping People Change.* Pergamon Press, Inc., 1975.

Knapp, M. *Social Intercourse: From Greeting to Goodbye.* Allyn and Bacon, Inc., 1978.

Luscher, Max. *The Color Test.* Pocket Books, 1971.

_____. *The Four Color Person.* Pocket Books, 1979.

_____. *Personality Signs.* Warner Books, 1981.

McCall, G., and J. L. Simmons. *Identities and Interactions.* The Free Press, 1966.

Maccoby, E., and Jacklin C. Maccoby. *The Psychology of Sex Differences.* Stanford University Press, 1974.

Meadow, Charles. *Sounds and Signals: How We Communicate.* Westminster Press, 1975.

Miller, G., ed. "Interpersonal Communication in Developing Acquaintance." *Exploration In Interpersonal Communication.* Sage, 1976.

_____. "Personal Relationships Research in the 1980's: Toward an Understanding of Complex Human Sociology." *Western Journal of Speech Communication* 44 (1 980): 114-19.

_____, ed. *Theory and Practice in Interpersonal Attraction.* Academic Press, 1977.

Molloy, John. *Dress for Success.* Warner Books, 1976.

_____. *Live for Success.* Perigord Press, 1981.

Nunnally, J. *Psychometric Theory.* McGraw-Hill, 1967.

Oliphant, Robert E. *Trial Techniques with Irving Younger.* National Practice Institute, 1981.

Pizer, Vernon. *You Don't Say: How People Communicate Without Speech.* Putnam, 1978.

Poiret, Maude. *Body Talk.* Award Books, 1970.

Rickers-Ovsiankina, M. A., and A. A. Kusmin. "Individual Differences in Social Accessibility." *Psychological Reports* 4 (1958): 391-406.

Sannito, Thomas, and Burke Arnolds. "Jury Results: The Factors at Work." *Trial Diplomacy Journal* (1982).

Scott, M., and W. Powers. *Interpersonal Communication: A Question of Needs.* Houghton Mifflin Co., 1978.

Sommer, Robert. *Personal Space.* Prentice Hall, Inc., 1969.

Time. September 1981.

Toffler, A. *Future Shock.* Random House, 1970.

Wheeler, L., and J. Nezlek. "Sex Differences in Social Participation." *Journal of Personality and Social Psychology* 35 (1971): 742-54.

Wilmot, W. *Dyadic Communications.* 2d ed. Addison-Wesley, 1979.

Zunin, L., and N. Zunin. *Contact: The First Four Minutes.* Balantine, 1972.

NOTES:

NOTES:

NOTES:

NOTES:

NOTES: